Why Can't I Just Be Happy? A Realistic Approach to Happiness

Why Can't I Just Be Happy? A Realistic Approach to Happiness

By

Rolf Nabb

Bright Yellow Hat

Why Can't I Just Be Happy? A Realistic Approach to Happiness
by
Rolf Nabb

Bright Yellow Hat
an imprint of New Tradition Books
ISBN 1932420320

For information contact:
Bright Yellow Hat
brightyellowhat@yahoo.com

For everybody.

Contents

Not happy? Well, why aren't you?

"Why can't I just be happy?"

We've all asked ourselves this question from time to time and we've all wondered why it's so hard. Considering that you probably include yourself in the vast majority of what I'll refer to as "us," you probably find yourself wondering this from time to time as well.

If there's anything that unites us as human beings, it's the desire to be happy. Sure, we all like to eat, sleep and do all the other necessary things that make us human beings, but sometimes it just doesn't work out for us. Sometimes, when our lives become complicated and harder to manage, we become vulnerable to despair and sadness. This is when we become helpless. This is when we become unhappy.

From my years of observation and talking to people, I've figured out that being a happy person is a pretty easy thing to accomplish if you can just set your sights on the right targets and get your priorities straight. However, we all occasionally seem to lose sight of what make us happy. Some of us get more off track than others and some of us lose our way completely. This is where this book comes in. I want to help you get back on track and, if you're already a happy person but want to be more consistent in your good mood, then this book should help you too.

But before we get much farther in talking about happiness, I think that it's important that we determine what it is.

I'll define it like this:
Happiness is the state of being where we experience joy.

This definition is a little broad, but it has to be. Happiness can occur in many situations and under many circumstances. It can happen because you win the lottery or because your favorite show is on. Regardless, the uniting factor is the experiencing of joy. The problem is that we let things get in the way of this joy and consequently become unhappy.

I am a firm believer that the reason that most people are unhappy is because they simply won't let themselves be happy. Of course, this sounds a little simplistic and clichéd, but it's true. A cliché is a cliché for a reason, right? Whether we delay our gratification, doubt ourselves, concentrate on what other people are doing or any of the countless other ways we have of sabotaging ourselves, it all boils down to the fact that we are taking the long way around every subject and ending up experiencing unhappiness. We lose focus of our basic needs and wants and wind up miserable.

Another problem we have with being happy is that we're just not in tune with the human condition. We waste time worrying about things that are just a normal part of life. We get hung up on this person or on that perfect job or whatever and we can't accept that sometimes things don't work out exactly as we would like. We think that we have to analyze the issue again and again until it makes us miserable.

One way we can overcome these issues is to realize that everything is not an ideal situation. This is a very important step to being much more content with life. If we can just learn to accept certain facts about ourselves and our lives just as we accept the fact that the sky is blue and the grass green, our outlook will be that much better. Of course, I will be addressing this in the book.

Now, of course, not everybody in the world is unhappy. I don't want to paint everyone with the same brush. Some people are always very happy and if they're not, they usually know how to cheer themselves up. Some people just have the knack. Some people just know what to do and how to avoid the pitfalls that most of us fall victim to. Let me tell you, it's not hard to be happy. But you can't take yourself too seriously. You're also going to have to learn a few things, most of which you already know but are too self-involved or introspective to see.

When I sat down to write this book, I had one goal and that was to help people understand that it's not such a hard thing to be happy. Regardless of what misery you've suffered or are suffering, if you can just step back and gain a little perspective, you'll see that you too can be happy. The obstacles we face are easy to overcome if you can just recognize them. Accept yourself, realize that you're not helpless and you'll be just fine. You're much stronger than you think.

Let's get started.

The happiest people on earth.

If we're going to discuss happiness, I think that it's important that we first take a look at people who are happy. Yes, as I mentioned in the previous chapter, it's true that some people are happier than others. As hard as it may be for us to believe, not everyone in the world is miserable. It's also true that we've all seen these happy people and wonder just why are they in such a good mood. They have good attitudes and a better outlook on life than they should. Or at least that's our opinion as outside observers. For some reason they aren't encumbered by the same problems of unhappiness as the rest of us. I've thought about it quite a bit and I figured out that the happiest people on earth share a few common characteristics. I don't think that this is a coincidence. There are common threads that run through their positive attitudes.

The happiest people on earth are usually:
- ✓ Not very self-aware.
- ✓ Not very self-conscious.
- ✓ Not deep thinkers.
- ✓ Aren't always searching for answers.
- ✓ Don't take themselves seriously.
- ✓ Live in the present.
- ✓ Know and accept their place in the world.
- ✓ Accept that they are never truly in control of things.

Now I'm sure that many of you have noticed these same things, but just haven't put two and two together. You probably see these people as simple. *As not intelligent.* While these descriptions may be partially accurate, they are not entirely true. I'm just saying that happy people share these characteristics. Simple people are not always happy just as intelligent people are not always miserable. Also, for the record, I am by no means suggesting that you should chuck your education and intelligence in order to chase some pipe dream of happiness. However, I do think that we should take some notes. We should just swallow our pride and realize that they might be able to teach us a thing or two. After all, they apparently instinctively know something that we don't.

This isn't something you see with the happiest people on earth because they are going more by their instincts that tell them what they have to do to be happy. Observe people in long lasting relationships. Observe parents who really love their children. Look at people who really enjoy their lives and aren't always striving for a promotion or trolling for a deal. These people are focused on the present. Sure they think about the future and plan for it, but they cannot exist for something that hasn't happened yet. They understand that life is not a game. They understand that it is the real thing and it should be appreciated as such. Sure, they may not be bungee jumping off the Empire State Building for a "rush" but they have other outlets that make them feel like they're living. They aren't sacrificing everything for something that may or may not happen in the future. They also realize that they aren't in control of anything when it comes to life. They take it as it comes and understand that they are just along for the ride. The reason why they don't take themselves so seriously in this regard is because they usually don't think that much about this kind of stuff. In other words, as I was saying earlier, they don't let their brains get in the way.

It's no strange wonder that when you watch television programs about bushmen in Africa or natives in South America, you can't help but notice but how happy they are. They are living in squalor without modern appliances and are barely scratching out a subsistence, but they smile easily and usually seem to be without a care in the world. They know what their place is in the world. They are fulfilling roles that have been defined over thousands of years. They aren't graduating from college and then stumbling around for the next ten years wondering if maybe they should have gotten a different degree. This just isn't in their mindset.

While it's good that we are all mavericks and like to do our own thing, I think this independence can also sometimes lead to problems. This is because that we, just like these so-called primitives, are also descended from groups with clearly defined roles. As a result, these free-wheeling tendencies can sometimes cause us to lose our way. We just don't know what to do anymore. It's those souls who have accidentally stumbled into something or are simply uncomplicated enough just to let things happen who have the market cornered on happiness.

If we could put this kind of happiness in a bottle then we wouldn't have a problem with so much disaffection and disenchantment. However we can't, so we'll just have to try to achieve it other ways. First, we have to stop thinking so much and start living our lives.

Worst case scenario thinking and the unhappiness of the overly analytical.

Now that we've discussed the happiest people on earth, let's discuss you, the person who is just a little more complicated. The person who is intelligent. The person who has a tendency to think too much. If the simplest people on earth are happy, then what makes the more intelligent people unhappy?

I hate to say this but usually the more intelligent a person is, the more miserable he is. This is not always the case, but most of the time it is. This can usually be attributed to the fact that intelligent people possess the creativity to see what they do not have and also the clarity to see that things can be better. However, what usually gets lost in the shuffle is the notion of how good things are at the present. This ability to assess a situation can lead to helplessness on our part because we can see just how overwhelming the world can be. Intelligent people look at everything from so many different angles that they always see all the worst case scenarios to such an extent that the best case scenarios get overlooked. I like to call it the *unhappiness of the overly analytical.* It can also be referred to as *worst case scenario thinking.*

Worst case scenario thinking is a thing we learned as children to cushion ourselves from disappointment. It's not necessarily a bad thing because it helps us solve problems and foresee potential difficulties down the road. However, what happens is that some of us apply it to every situation to such an extent that all the joy is sucked out. We're so concerned about things going badly or we become, in a sense, *locked up* in our thinking. As a result, we find ourselves unable to do anything because we are so crippled due to our fears that something will go wrong. If you're guilty of this kind of thinking, you're going to have to make a conscious effort to emphasize the best case scenarios when you're "analyzing" a situation. You probably don't even think in terms of best case scenarios, do you? Well, you're going to have to start. Not everything is all bad. You just think it is. Stop being a worst case scenario thinker. You'll be surprised at how your world opens up.

Remember over-intellectualizing does not necessarily mean that you're actually figuring anything out. The next time you find yourself thinking exclusively in terms of worst case scenarios, make a conscious effort to come up with some best case scenarios as well. Don't fall victim to the unhappiness of the overly analytical.

What causes people to be unhappy?

If the answer was as simple as the question, then you wouldn't be reading this book, would you? You would be out chasing rainbows and grinning from ear to ear at everybody you see. Of course, I'm just being facetious, but you get my point.

While all the ideas that we've discussed contribute to unhappiness, they usually just serve to assist it. They are like *unhappiness accessories*. They enhance rather than cause the problem. The actual cause is much more direct and easier to pin down. I think biggest thing that causes people to be unhappy is when they're powerless to make things go their way. In other words, when it becomes obvious to them that they are not in control of their world.

It sounds like a fairly simple explanation, but it's not. It addresses issues of loss of control, bad childhoods, bad relationships, you name it. It encompasses everything. For example, let's say that your life is just blah and you're unhappy because of it. It's not that your life is blah that you're unhappy. You're unhappy because your life is blah and you think you can't do anything about it. If you could do something about it, your unhappiness would be more like a momentary discomfort. You would know that you'll get past it, you just haven't yet. The same thing goes with bad relationships. Maybe you're unhappy because you're dating a loser, yet dropping him leaves you still unhappy. It's not because you're alone, it's because you're powerless to obtain what you perceive as your "ideal" situation.

This feeling of helplessness is what you need to focus on when you're unhappy. Many times, you can actually do something to remedy your situation, but through social conditioning and worst-case scenario thinking you think you're powerless to change anything. You have to realize that you always have power to change your outcome. You can always do something. The key is to not feel overwhelmed. Remember, you're bigger than any situation.

If you can just recognize that the reason why you're unhappy is because you think you're powerless, it will be only a matter of time before your confidence will grow.

When you're feeling down, take the following actions:
- ✓ Step back and assess the situation.
- ✓ Key in why you think you're powerless.
- ✓ Think about what you can do to change your situation.
- ✓ Formulate a plan.
- ✓ Make it happen.

At first your plan to change your situation may not be successful, but don't despair. Now you know what you have to do (make an effort to change things), you'll eventually figure out a way to fix it. I'm not saying it's easy, but it's not as hard as you think.

If you can overcome your feelings of helplessness, you will be able to beat your unhappiness. Everybody feels bad about something at some time. This is only human. The difference is that some people know that it's not permanent. These people are the ones that we consider to be the happy ones. They know that whatever problem they have is just a temporary burden they have to endure until things get better. Just accept that things will sometimes go bad for you, but also sometimes things will go well. And now that you know the root feeling behind your unhappiness, there's nothing to stop you from moving forward. Remember you're not helpless to change your situation unless you let yourself be.

What can I do to not be unhappy?

I'm sure you're thinking that this is a bit of a convoluted chapter title, aren't you? Well, there's a reason for that. I'm not putting forth the question of how can you be happy, but rather how can you not be unhappy because I think that it's impossible for anyone to be happy all of the time.

Yes, you read that right. I don't think that people can be happy all of the time. Sure, some of us are happier than others just as some of us are unhappier than others, but generally speaking, the most well-adjusted people usually fall somewhere in between. Their feelings usually fall on the happy side of the middle with occasional and brief forays into the unhappy side of things. An easier way to look at this is to realize that the people we consider happy are happy most of the time but not always.

The thing to realize is that it's impossible to maintain the intensity that extreme happiness brings without sometimes dive-bombing into misery. Have you ever noticed the highs and lows that people in intense relationships experience? Perhaps you've experienced them yourself. You're so happy that you've met this amazing person that you just want to give him/her the world. However when he/she does something that may not live up to your expectations, your mood quickly turns sour. You absolutely can't stand him/her anymore. Of course this feeling is temporary until you get over it. This is exactly the kind of stuff I'm talking about.

So, what can you do to not be unhappy?

It's simple. Accept things as they are and just go with it. Find the good things in everyday occurrences. If you can step back and see the big picture, you can get a better perspective and see that things aren't really that bad. Sure, you may have been taken advantage of by some person, but you're not the only one. Sure you may have wasted your money on some sort of foolishness, but rest assured that you're not the first person who has ever done this. All you have to remember in these circumstances is that you must vow to do better in the future. You will recover from these unfortunate events. This is called learning. Each challenge you face will only help you to grow and become stronger.

One thing that's helped me in life is something I overheard a particularly level-headed person say one time. In regards to some very stressful events that were transpiring in the workplace and causing everyone around him to stress, he said, *"I'm not worried. It'll work out one way or another."* Sure, this may at first sound like a facetious remark, but just think about it. Things will work out how they're supposed to work out regardless of what we do. All we can do is our best. We can't shape fate; however, we can give it our all and hope everything turns out well. We cannot control the world. Just as unhappiness is caused from a lack of control, *even more unhappiness is caused by trying to gain control over things that we can't possibly control.* We have to recognize that we, as human beings, can only do so much and that we are only in control of ourselves. After we have given our best, it is out of our hands. We can't "body-english" an event such as a wonderful relationship, or a promotion into happening. After we have done our part, we are done. All we can do is hope for the best.

This is what it takes to not be unhappy.

Being levelheaded is the goal here, not some sort of deluded wide-eyed return to childish ignorance. Face it. We're not going to ever go back to that point in our lives. The only way that this is possible is if we turn senile or something catastrophic happens and we lose our minds. I don't think that these are good options. You just have to accept things as they are and make the most of them. Maybe your life didn't turn out the way you wanted, however it turned out the way it was supposed to. Maybe you didn't get into the college of your choice. Maybe you didn't make a big splash in Hollywood. Maybe you got pregnant in high school, therefore shattering your dreams of Olympic glory. You have to accept that maybe it wasn't your place to have Olympic glory. This much should be obvious because it clearly did not work out in this way. If it was supposed to have happened, then the gold medal would be displayed on your wall now. But that's not to say your role in life is not important. Maybe it was your place to give birth to the person who would achieve this. Maybe it was your place to give someone else encouragement and advice. Maybe it was your place to show others what you learned from your own mistakes. I firmly believe that everybody has a role in life and the problem is that most of us don't know what it is and/or don't accept it. If people would open their eyes and see their situation clearly, they would be much happier.

So, in regards to the question of what can you do to not be unhappy—just go with the flow. Accept your place in the world and do your best. This is important to obtaining happiness. Also don't try to control things over which you have no power.

Other than that, there's not much you can do. Except be miserable, that is.

The different types of people.

One problem I have with most books that try to tell people how to be happy is that for the most part, all they do is give people ways to fool themselves into simply acting happy. I know that they mean well, but I think that it takes more than self-affirmation and asserting your personhood to make someone truly believe that he or she is a good person. Looking at the glass as half-full rather half-empty is good for changing those negative habits, but does this truly reach the core of a person's unhappiness? I don't think so. I think that it takes more than that.

You're probably asking what makes me think that I know better, right? Well, what I know is this. We work best when we're able to categorize things. We have to know what things are called and where to put them. If we can't define something then it is extremely hard for us to understand it. That's why I have broken down the population into three groups by using their dispositions. This will better illustrate what I'm talking about and also help you understand what sort of person you are.

Here are the three groups:
- ✓ People who are happy.
- ✓ People who are unhappy (the chronically miserable).
- ✓ People who are neither.

People who are happy.

The first category of people is where I think most of us are. It's just a matter of how much we allow ourselves to be happy. We recognize that we want to be happy. We recognize when we are happy, but we might not be cognizant of what makes us happy. We just sort of bounce into happy situations. While we may not be happy all the time, we certainly know the feeling of happiness and we know enough to recognize that it's a good place to be. These are the people who are reading this book. They know it's out there, but they just can't seem to get there as much as they want. These people may be sad now, but they were once happy. They just want to find that place again. This group is also chock full of people who are won't let themselves be happy because they are waiting for something better to come along. Something that will *allow* them to be happy. Something that gives them an excuse to be happy.

People who are unhappy.

People who are truly unhappy are probably not going to be reading this book. Truly unhappy people are usually so full of themselves and so ego-driven that nothing that anybody can do or say will help them. They have to reach the conclusion themselves and usually they may become happy on their own. This usually happens when some life changing event happens in their lives. They may have a child, a close shave with death or a religious experience. Everybody knows these people. Everybody knows someone who is so chronically miserable that it just sucks the energy out of you just being around them. You can only hope that these people see the light early on enough to have a somewhat enjoyable life. If not, they're going to be spending a lot of time alone.

People who are neither.

This third group is dull to the world. They go through life without much emotion and have a generally blah attitude towards everything. They experience highs and lows that are generally short lived and quickly go towards the middle. The bad thing for these people is that because they don't fully appreciate the good things in their lives, they can barely handle when bad things happen to them. They have a hard time when extremely bad circumstances happen to them because they have never developed the proper coping devices. These people wouldn't be reading this book either because there's no need. They just really don't see the point.

Of course, I know that there are more than three categories of people in the world, but I have developed these three generalizations for the sake of easy illustration. A book about happiness is going to be read by happy people who either don't quite know how to achieve consistent happiness or they want to learn how to be even happier. No matter how miserable you are, if you read a book like this, then that is a sure indicator that you are a happy person struggling to be the person you truly are. It's that simple.

Now that you know you're a happy person, don't you feel a lot better about yourself? A lot happier, perhaps? Once you know what kind of a person you are and know that you do have the potential to be happy (everybody does) then it's much easier to move on and get started. Unhappiness is baggage that is very easily dropped if you just know how to let go of it. Also, you have to know that most of the time, if you just take a look around, you would realize that you're already pretty happy. That is to say, if you would just let yourself relax and feel it.

The fear of being happy.

But can there be such a thing, you ask? Of course. There's a fear of everything else, isn't there? Why should this be any different?

The fear of being happy occurs when people think that they are not entitled to be happy. They look around at others who have less than them or more difficult lives and think that they have no reason to be in a better state. They are also afraid that if they are happy, then something bad will happen to them as a result. They think that they will be punished for being happy. They feel like the world is in such a balance that if they become happy about something then something bad will have to happen to equalize the situation.

But how can you overcome this?

The way to deal with the fear of being happy is to understand that you are not the center of the universe. You are not some galactic linchpin whose emotions must be weighed and measured in order to achieve the cosmic order. There is more than enough happiness to go around in the world and you will never take more than your fair share. You should realize that you are just a person who lives and loves just like everybody else. Sure, bad things may happen to you, but it's not because you were happy about something else. It was just because they were meant to happen. You cannot connect the dots when it comes to these situations. Remember, you can't control the world. You can only control yourself.

So, the next time you feel a guilty little twinge when something good happens to you, just remember that it's okay for you to feel good. Happiness is not a zero sum game. Just because you're happy doesn't mean that someone else is unhappy. It also doesn't mean that something bad is going to happen to you later on. All it means is that something good happened for you and you should enjoy it.

Fooling yourself is not enough.

As I mentioned before, there are self-help techniques that are, for the most part, simply ways that allow you to easily fool yourself into a false sense of happiness without doing anything to fix the root problem—your attitude. While it's important to get into the habit of being happy, if you don't fix the core problem, you're going to be in a constant struggle. Also, one of the most important things to accept is the recognition of the fact that you will not be happy all the time. This is okay. There is no need to fool yourself otherwise. There are things that will happen which will give you a genuine excuse to be unhappy. However, if you fix your attitude and perspective, you will be able to weather these situations and achieve equilibrium much more easily than a person who hasn't.

"But how do I fix my attitude?" I'm sure that this is the next question.

It's actually quite easy to do, but because it is so easy, it is made out to be much more difficult than it actually is.

What you have to do is:
- ✓ Appreciate what you have.
- ✓ Recognize that you are just a human with human faults.
- ✓ Stand up for yourself when you have to.

- ✓ Always do your best in any situation, but recognize that your best may not be good enough. If this is the case then it wasn't meant to be. Accept this and move on.
- ✓ Understand that it's okay to fail as long as you make a good effort.
- ✓ Be the best *you* that you can be.
- ✓ Don't delay your happiness.
- ✓ Don't live in the future.
- ✓ Don't live in the past.
- ✓ Don't try to live like the people in the movies.
- ✓ Don't dwell on your bad childhood.

This is the biggest one:
- ✓ Concentrate on the core things that make humans happy:
  - Enough to eat.
  - Comfort.
  - Love.
  - Good experiences.

If you can concentrate on these steps, happiness will follow. Most of the time when people aren't happy or aren't as happy as they could be, it's because their expectancy doesn't match up with reality. They are always left wanting for more. They are always left disappointed. You cannot expect the best out of every situation. While it would be nice if everything always worked out to your advantage, it probably won't. So just try to be reasonable. Following these simple steps will get you into the habit of being happier and more realistic. They will also get you on the road to changing your attitude. Of course, it's not just a matter of flicking a switch, but over time, careful reflection and self examination will help you to change your mindset. Self-help techniques, while being well-meaning, are usually just gimmicks that ultimately end up being lampooned because of their silliness. I'm not saying that they don't always work, because if a person truly wants to improve his attitude, he will do it. I just think that if a person doesn't rely on gimmicks, he'll have an easier time making progress.

Once again, don't try to use gimmicks to fool yourself into being happy. Try to concentrate on the core things that truly make you feel good and learn to deal with the things that make you feel bad. I know that it's not necessarily easy, however, it is a lot simpler than you think.

Delayed gratification. What are we waiting for?

No matter how you look at it, the concept of delayed gratification is a major obstacle to our happiness. Well, maybe not delayed gratification itself, but a misguided notion of it that we probably developed somewhere in childhood.

It's true. It applies to all of us. We're all waiting for something, right? Whether it's a new car, a new house, a new job or Mr. or Ms. Right, we just can't ever seem to let ourselves relax and take advantage of what we currently have. What usually happens when we are in a constant state of anticipation is that we end up waiting for the one thing that we most desire: happiness. This is especially true today with the idea of that something better is going to come along if we're just patient enough. Don't get too used to the way things are now, because they're going to change…for the better!

We all know that this isn't necessarily true. Sure, one can be an eternal optimist, but there's only so much delayed gratification even the most positive of individuals can take before he turns bitter and gives up on the world. In order to be happy, a person has to find the perfect balance between optimism and practicality and appreciate what's going on in the here and now.

I see it everyday and I've been guilty of it myself. For some reason, there is an innate quality in humans that we are always willing to give up what's pleasant in the present for something that may possibly be better in the future. This is also true in the animal kingdom. Just watch a dog during mealtime when he's offered the possibility of something better to eat. It doesn't matter if he's eating filet mignon; he'll gladly drop it for the unknown allure of day-old luncheon loaf.

Of course, this example is a bit ham-fisted and general, but you get the point. While in the case of the dog, the better thing is a possibility of something material. This is just a fact of life when it comes to material things, and sometimes, you do have to risk what you have in order to get something better. This is particularly true of investing in stocks or starting a new job; however, this isn't the point of the chapter. No, what I'm talking about is more substantial. I'm talking about intangibles like happiness and peace of mind.

It's simple to see when this flawed thinking first occurred. Most of us learned the lessons from childhood well. We were told that we had to wait to be happy. We were told that we had to wait until we were finished with dinner before we could have dessert. We were told that we had to wait until we had our homework finished before we could play or watch TV. We were told that we had to wait until summer to go on vacation. Then, as we got older and started going to church we were told that we had to suffer here on earth in order to go to our great reward in the afterlife. All this is well and good, but somehow, I think that this idea of delayed gratification has gotten transferred to almost every aspect of our lives. This is especially true when it comes to our careers and relationships. The situation isn't helped by TV shows that emphasize the joys of being eternally single. What people fail to notice is that, in their real lives, actors and actresses in these television shows rarely follow the example of their characters. Most are married with children. Most of them enjoy their careers and aren't waiting on something better to come along.

Time is fleeting and there are many of us who just can't accept the fact that there is a present because we're too busy living in the future. I'm talking about people who will never commit to a relationship because there is the faint possibility that a better guy or gal is just around the corner waiting for them to show up. Can't settle too soon, because Mr. Right is a-waitin'! The problem is that, many times, Mr. Right never has a chance to materialize because he's isn't given a chance to prove himself. Oh well, there's always the future, right? This isn't necessarily always the case.

There are many readers who will think that this book is just an attempt to get people to settle, to give up and just accept whatever squalid circumstances they find themselves in. This isn't true. I think that people should always try to better themselves. Not every relationship or job is a good one. Some should definitely be dropped. All I'm trying to do is make you aware of the fact that you may be taking your present for granted and in the process, delaying your happiness. Perhaps indefinitely.

The thing to pick up on here is that if you delay your happiness long enough, there's a possibility that you'll develop a habit of always delaying it. You may even delay it so long that you lose track of what it is that makes you happy.

Hey, here's an idea. If you must delay something, why not delay your unhappiness? There's no hard and fast rule that says you only have to wait on the good things.

The fear of being ordinary.

When it comes to our emotional well-being, there's a fear that dominates us and causes us so much misery, it's absolutely overwhelming. It has led to some people spending their lives in a state of bitterness and others living lives of heartbreak and regret. It is big, but yet so silly when you think about it, it's really hard to fathom why it has such a grip on us. So what is this fear, you ask? What is it that absolutely paralyzes us throughout our lives, from the time we are born to the time we're laid to rest? It may seem ridiculous, but we're all afraid of being ordinary.

From the time we are children, we are taught that in order to be a valuable member of society, we have to stand out. We have to show ourselves to be apart from the pack. However, curiously enough, we also despise those who do stand out and are not ordinary. It's an odd situation that only serves to make us doubt and dislike ourselves. It also causes us more unhappiness than we need.

Just why is it that we fear being ordinary? Is it because it makes us more of a number than a name? Is it because we're taught by the movies, magazines and TV that in order to be somebody, we have to be something more than normal? Is it because we all want to be special? I think that that the answer lies in all these statements. We are taught from the media that the wilder and crazier we are, the more attention we'll get. We all want to be individuals and we all want to be special. All these are natural, normal desires.

What is not normal is the high amount of discomfort we feel with ourselves when we realize that we are truly ordinary and normal. That we may not necessarily stand out in a crowd.

Well, what I want to know is what is so wrong with being ordinary? The answer is obvious. Nothing.

What we need to realize is that ordinary is good. It means that we are in a good state where nothing bad is happening to us. It means that things are going smoothly. Sure, we're not winning the Nobel Peace Prize, but who is? Most people who are not ordinary would do anything to be normal. There are people with medical conditions who would be as happy as anything to have the house and white picket fence. We need to look to their wish for normalcy to appreciate what we truly have. Being ordinary is desired because to be truly different is not necessarily a good thing.

Just ask someone who isn't and they'll tell you.

Sure you want to be special, but the thing about it is that you already are. Everyone is special. You have unique DNA, don't you? You are not like anybody else in the universe, are you? Do you really need your own TV show to be special? Do you really need to jump out of an airplane in order to be unique?

You can't help it. You are special and you are an individual and you will be even more of one if you'll just accept that you are an ordinary person just like everybody else. Even people you think of as being extraordinary are usually only extraordinary in a very limited number of ways. Aside from the thing that makes them stand out, they are just like everybody else. And truth be known, you probably have something that you can do extraordinarily, it's just that it may not be as high profile as some of the more famous people. Just think about it long enough and I know that you'll figure out what it is that you can do better than just about everybody you know. You may be a great cook. You may be a great parent. Talent comes in many different packages. You just have to figure out which one is yours.

So, the next time you're feeling a little down about being ordinary, just remember that it's good to be ordinary, and that you're probably a lot more special than you think. Ordinary is not boring and the sooner you can realize this, the happier you'll be.

We can't let our dreams get in the way.

As I mentioned before, helplessness is the underlying element, but there are many, many more things that can be stumbling blocks to our happiness. We've already discussed our ingrained delayed gratification, but this is just a part of the story. Directly related to this is the fact that we sometimes let our dreams get in the way of feeling good about ourselves. We fixate so much on what we want in the future that we forget what it is that we need right now.

It's good to have something to aspire to, to have dreams, but when they are unrealistic and get in the way of living a full life, then there's a problem. For example, I know a young lady who has had the dream of being a famous actress for as long as she can remember. She moved to Los Angeles and has done everything she can to achieve this goal. While she is very talented, she hasn't had the kind of luck or made the right connections that she needs to accomplish anything big. However, that's not the problem. The problem is that her dream is so ingrained in her that she refuses to look at any other options in her life. She doesn't date that much because she doesn't want to be distracted from her craft. She hasn't ever tried to get any sort of serious job because she doesn't want to do anything that might divert her time and attention from any potential upcoming roles. Marriage is completely out of the question and she has never considered having children because of the strain that they would cause on her auditioning. She is perpetually in a state of readiness so that when her ship comes in she will be ready, bags packed and able to go away at a moment's notice. This is all well and good and I hope she achieves her goal, but she doesn't even realize that by focusing on this one thing in the future, she has completely overlooked the present. She is approaching forty and is probably one of the unhappiest people I know. She hasn't even stopped to consider where she is in her life because "it's going to happen, soon. I can feel it."

It's good to have dreams, but if we let them interfere with our happiness, then what good are they? We are constantly bombarded by messages of sticking to our dream and not settling for less. This is good, but I think that many of us do not listen with a discerning ear. We take these as excuses to not let ourselves experience a full range of living now in order to stay vigilant for whatever may come along.

Just think of it this way. When you see a homeless guy singing on the street corner, do you want to commend him for not giving up on his dream? Or do you think that he's pathetic? I think you get my point here. Of course, we were taught from childhood that we always had to do something unpleasant in order to achieve something that we liked, but we were never told that we had to do something unpleasant to be happy. This is something that we've created ourselves. I think that we all have something of the martyr in us when it comes to this subject and we just can't stop suffering in the now to be happy in the future.

I think that another one of the reasons for people suffering is because they haven't quite figured out how things work. They are ignorant of the process. Like in the publishing and entertainment industry, for example. People strive for years and never accomplish anything. It is because they have no talent? Not necessarily. It's because the process is largely out of their hands and until they learn how things work, they are simply barking up the wrong tree. This can sometimes takes years, decades even. This is why is it is so important for you not to abandon your life for a career. Sure, it may happen, but when?

One important thing to remember is that *nothing is as valuable as something in the future, until it's unattainable in the past.* This includes your life as well as material things.

As I keep repeating, don't think that I'm telling you to settle for less, because I'm not. I'm just saying that you should settle for what truly satisfies you. My advice to all you dreamers is that you should continue to dream and shoot for the stars, but remember that you sometimes have to step aside and figure out if your quest for success is right for you. Sometimes, it's good to switch paths. You know when something isn't working; you just have to listen to your own heart.

It's good to be a dreamer, just don't forget to live.

What-if versus What-is. You have to have something to look forward to.

Just as there are little things that can add to your unhappiness, the reverse is also true. There are things that you can do to help you become happier. Having something to look forward to is one of the most powerful.

It's true. If you've ever noticed, one of the most common defining features of happy people is that they have something to look forward to. They have a reason to get up in the morning. They have a reason not to chuck it all and move into a monastery. They know that there is something better down the road for them and they can't wait to get started.

"Now, just wait a second here!" A voice from the audience asks. "But aren't you contradicting yourself? I thought that we weren't supposed to delay our gratification? I thought that you said that we should live in the now?"

Well, I'm not doing anything of the sort. If you'll read closely, you'll see that I'm not saying that people should wait for something to come along to look forward to. I'm saying that *they have something to look forward to in the here and now.* They already have an appreciation of what they have and what they've achieved. They have a good relationship to come home to. They have kids they want to see. They have a job that they enjoy. If you want to be happy, looking forward to something can be a big boost. It doesn't even have to be anything big. In fact, it can be anything, just so long as it's tangible and it doesn't involve either playing mind games or not appreciating what you currently have.

Just think how you feel when you have something exciting to do. Maybe you're going on a cruise. Maybe you're going to the big game. It's a feeling of joyous anticipation because you bought your ticket and know that you are definitely going. Contrast this with how you feel when you go out on a date with somebody you've been seeing for a few days and still aren't sure about. Sure, he's nice, but what about the guy that you keep running into at work? Maybe this isn't working out after all…

You see what I mean? It's the difference between anticipation and *what if*. In the first example there's expectancy while in the second there's the resignation that nothing in the present is going to be as good as something in the future.

While having something to look forward to may not always make you happy every day of your life, it will certainly smooth out the rough spots. The solution is to replace the idea of *what-if* with *what-is*. Appreciate what you have and you will always have something to look forward to.

True optimism. Acceptance is the key.

Did you ever get the feeling that you weren't getting the whole story? Well, when it comes to your happiness, I think that this is definitely the case.

Here's why: Many of the so-called experts out there are always going on about how a person needs to accept himself in order to be happy. He has to make peace with himself and all his mistakes and foibles. In other words, he has to be true to himself. While, I'm not one to disagree with this, I think that it's not quite the whole story. This stuff is very important in your quest for happiness, but accepting yourself is only part of the equation. Accepting the fact that you have a limited ability to control your universe is a much more important aspect.

I know that I will be called a defeatist or a pessimist for saying such a thing, but I firmly believe it's true. If you want to be happy, you will have to accept that things can go wrong and that you will mess up occasionally. You have to be on an even keel where you can handle both the highs and lows that life brings. While some people may think that I have a negative outlook, I say that they're wrong. I suggest that such an outlook is very positive. It is truly optimistic because even though I realize that things may not always work out for the best, I know that they will not always work out for the worst either. I can maintain a good attitude even though I accept the fact that a situation can go pear-shaped at any moment. All I can do is my best and hope for things to turn out well. This is true optimism. The cheerleader-style-rah-rah positive attitudes that are turned out by various self-help seminars and TV talk shows are just new paint on an old barn. The internal dialogue hasn't changed. A person who goes this route is the same person except now he has a big smile plastered on his face. It's no wonder that when reality sets in and bad things start happening, the person who takes this route usually falls more deeply into negative thinking than he already was.

If you can accept that you are not perfect, then it will be relatively easy to accept that the world isn't perfect either. You have to accept that while there is an order to the world, it may not make sense to you. For example, if you work all your life to be a writer, there's no guarantee that your hard work is going to pay off monetarily. However, the process of writing might help you in other ways. You just have to be open enough to understand that x multiplied by y does not always equal xy because there are many more variables out there than you can possibly realize.

Another way of looking at it is in terms of movie storylines. Many people (me included) have a tendency to think like this. We think that there is always going to be a logical resolution to every situation. We think that everything is going to work out for the best. It's only natural that we think this way because we have been inadvertently programmed to do this because we watch a lot of TV and movies. I have seen this kind of TV/movie influenced thinking happen on many different occasions. I remember when the OJ trial was going on, a lady I worked with would watch the trial religiously. Every day she would have a new theory about who did it. She would concoct complex motivations and scenarios for all the major and minor players in the trial and, in effect, was turning it into a virtual whodunit. She didn't realize it, but, in her mind, she was treating a very real situation like it was a TV show. Now, most of us don't go quite that far in our thinking, but it's easy to see that I'm making a valid point here. Unlike a movie, life does not always have a logical conclusion other than death. We just need to realize that we will have to play it by ear most of the time.

Let's get this straight. I'm not saying that a person should have a negative view of the world, but rather a realistic one. Life is too short to be depressed because things aren't working out the way you thought they would. Things work out the way they are supposed to and you just have to accept it. You can assuage any doubt by always trying to do your best in all endeavors. It's also very important to note that while bad things do happen in life, good things happen too. You just have to accept everything. Life isn't always a bowl of cherries, but then again it's not always the pits either.

Accepting the world and its complexities is the key to happiness and it will open up your mind to many other areas of thought. Once you can understand that you cannot understand the world, then you're free to stop worrying about trying to control everything in your life. You will be able to appreciate the good things with more enthusiasm and accept the bad things without collapsing. I'm not saying you should deaden yourself to the world, but just recognize the tenuous place you hold. Many people don't appreciate the good things that life has to offer because they think that they are the norm. They take them for granted and don't appreciate them until they're gone. They don't see the whole picture. Especially when it comes to themselves.

So what if you had an unhappy childhood?

One of the obstacles most of us face when it comes to our happiness and sense of well-being is our unhappy childhoods. Most people cannot break free from their bad childhood experiences and, as a result, continue to let these long past events and traumas influence them in their everyday attitudes and behaviors. They seem to be stagnated in their lives because of their bad childhoods.

Before we go any further, I'm going to dispel a common myth regarding the concept of childhood. I see this misconception especially in people who grew up in very dysfunctional homes and I think that it only makes the situation worse.

I hope your world doesn't collapse when I tell you this, but there is no such thing as an ideal childhood.

You heard me. I know you watch television and see people having ideal childhoods. I'm sure that you also remember your good friend who received a new bicycle every year for Christmas as having an ideal childhood. But this is not an accurate perception. Everybody has problems and while some childhood experiences are better than others, no one escapes childhood without some sort of unhappiness. Accept this and you will be better off for it.

If you are to be happy, you're going to have to break free from the concept of the ideal childhood. I know that this is easier said than done. Many people medicate themselves with reality numbing drugs so they can't feel the pain (or anything else for that matter). While it's a hard mountain to climb, overcoming your bad childhood is possible. Just like everything else I've mentioned in this book, the answer is in the acceptance. You have to accept what happened to you and then accept that you are no longer a child. You also have to realize that your parents may have done the best they could under the circumstances. Sure, they may not have been the greatest parents in the world, but maybe they were only using the tools given to them by their parents. Remember, you don't have a monopoly on the bad childhood market. If your parents weren't that great, chances are that theirs were even worse.

It's true that many children have suffered horrors so great that they will never forget—and probably shouldn't forget so they can pass on their experience to others for the benefit of future generations—what happened to them. It's also true that much of their unhappiness comes from the guilt associated with these horrors. They feel somehow at fault for what happened to them. It's understandable why people think this way. After all, why else would anybody do this kind of stuff to them? But this is a child's mind view. In their adult mind they know that they weren't at fault, but somehow can't quite overcome that hurdle in completely convincing themselves of this. While they understand, they just can't make themselves accept that there was nothing wrong with them and they didn't "bring it on themselves." They weren't inadequate or "not good enough."

Sometimes it's very hard to convince yourself of something you already know. However, once you start accepting the situation, you'll start listening to yourself and see the situation as it really was.

I also realize that many of you probably weren't physically abused as children but had parents who either were too busy or didn't seem to care. I know that when you look at this from your child's mind perspective, it still hurts. You realize that at that time in your life, you really needed nurturing and caring and it was in short supply. This keeps you from growing out of that wounded child phase and stunts your growth. The good news is that it's never too late for you to have that love you long desired, whether it's from a relationship, a child or yourself. You can find it if you can just get past the idea that you are a person who deserves it.

Once again, I stress the only way to overcome any bad childhood is to accept what happened and make peace with it. Realize that you were just a child and you were not responsible for the behavior of others. You must also accept the fact that you're an adult now. Your childhood has passed. While you were shaped by your childhood, your outlook in life is not wholly a result of it. You're seeking happiness, aren't you?

If you can just look objectively at your past and understand that you did the best you could do under the circumstances, you will be okay. Sure, you look at yourself now and think "but if I had had a loving father…" and "if my mother had…" But what good does that do? You are going to have to stop this. This kind of thinking is just going to make you both angry and unhappy. Besides, you don't know if things would have turned out any differently had your parents been a little bit better to you. You have to realize that you are a good, decent person regardless of what you think your childhood preordained. Sure, you may have made mistakes in the past because you didn't learn some essential lessons in childhood, but you learned them eventually, didn't you? So what if you've had a few screw ups. Who hasn't?

Once you let go of the idea of the perfect childhood, you can finally realize that no one is perfect and that none of us can achieve or have ever achieved this mythic state. We all make mistakes, just as our parents made mistakes with us. We all have skeletons in our closet and we all could have done better in certain circumstances if we had only had a little more knowledge, training, etc. And we could have all had better childhoods.

I know at this point, you're probably thinking, "But what if I had a happy childhood, but am still unhappy?" I say that this is a good thing and you should count yourself lucky. You should appreciate your childhood even more because many people out there aren't so fortunate. Your unhappiness is going to be easier to fix because it's not as ingrained. I say that if you had a happy childhood, you should be patting yourself on the back for having enough perception to recognize it.

Overcoming your bad childhood is tough, but if you can accept it as is, and understand that you weren't responsible for any shortcomings that may have happened in your upbringing, you will be on the road to happiness. If you can accept this, then you can accept the fact that you aren't perfect and that you will make mistakes. You will also be able to accept that you won't always be happy. And you will understand that you won't always be unhappy either. Accepting your childhood, good or bad, is vital to being happy. Once you begin to understand this concept, you are well on your way.

But I had such a good childhood. What happened?

While some people may have had terrible childhoods because of abusive, neglectful or aloof parents, there are those of us who had great childhoods. Some of us were so happy when we were children that the rest of our lives is a letdown. Our only happy memories come from childhood. These are the people whose adult lives is epilogue. What can people with happy childhoods do to be happy adults?

The answer to this question is practically the same as it is for everybody else except you have to work in reverse. A person has to come to terms with the fact that unhappiness strikes all people equally. It's true that some folks are happy as adults because they had happy childhoods, but this isn't always the case. Don't beat yourself up if you're not living up to the standards that you set as a child. You have to remember that children are geared for fun and happiness. They don't know any differently. They can be entertained by anything. You can't help the fact that things became demystified and boring as you got older. Stop beating yourself up over it and stop living in the past. The thing to do when you're thinking about how wonderful things were when you were a child is to think about why they were so wonderful. Try to remember the excitement you felt when you were experiencing things for the first time. You can't recapture the innocence but you can remember it.

I don't want anyone to think that I'm advocating anything controversial like regressive therapy or past life experiences because I'm not. All I'm saying is to remember the way you felt when you knew you were going to visit your grandparents or going to a fair. I know that I would be so excited about going places and doing things that I would almost be shaking. I wouldn't be able to sleep for days because I was excited about going to an amusement park. Remembering this feeling will be like a booster shot and will energize you in finding new endeavors and appreciating what you're doing now.

Another thing that adds to the unhappiness that occurs after childhood is that this is when we learned to take ourselves seriously. I'm sure that you remember this, too. Sure, as children we played and acted silly, but at some point we had to grow up and get serious. This is good. We can't act like children all our lives. However, when we start becoming so grown up that we think that we can no longer have fun, we are asking for the breakdown to occur. We long for those carefree days that we think can never happen again. This leads to helplessness that then spirals into unhappiness.

It's like this: People certainly don't have any trouble dwelling on the bad stuff in life, do they? So why not make it a priority to remember the good stuff? This just doesn't apply to your childhood but anything that made you happy. If you can do this, you can get a better idea of what it is that makes you feel good inside. You can more easily see the times in life where things went right and this will make it easier to repeat them.

So can you be as happy in adulthood as you were in childhood? Maybe. Maybe not, but you sure can try. Just like you can't live in the future, you can't live in the past either, but you can try to remember what made it great and then make every effort to make it happen again. Now.

You're not in high school anymore.

As I keep saying, if you want to be happy, there's a lot of stuff you're going to have to get over. One of these is that fact that you're not in high school anymore.

It's true that if you're like most of us, you probably didn't have that great of a time in high school. You were probably ostracized or belittled for whatever reason. Maybe your parents still treated you like a baby. Maybe you were a little more awkward at your awkward stage than the other kids. Maybe you were just a dweeb. Whatever it was, you're just going to have to get it through your head that that time is over. It's time to start living in the now.

But it's hard to get over those old hurts, right?

Of course it is. You'll never forget the humilities you suffered while you were in school. And you shouldn't. However, you do need to accept what happened. You need to understand that while you were picked on and abused, you were the core person you are now. The only problem was that nobody could see it. You hadn't come out of your shell yet. You were not quite *the you* that you were to become.

So what if your stomach ties in knots whenever you go to the supermarket and happen to see some of the people who used to pick on you? This is actually good therapy for you. When you see how they aren't quite as great as they were in high school, it's quite a demystifying experience. It really puts things into perspective when you see the captain of the football team buying toilet paper or befuddled in the produce aisle. You'll see that while they were once like gods walking upon the earth, they now have problems just like everyone else. While you shouldn't triumph in others' misfortunes, you can at least see that these people who looked down on you from their lofty places are just as human as you. You just need to get your mind out of that place in the past when you felt insignificant. You're a more confident person now. Smile and act like nothing happened. I can't promise you that these people feel bad about what they did to you because it's possible that they don't. Some do, but we don't live in an ideal world where people change. Regardless, don't let yourself fall into any of your old victimized patterns of thinking. Approach the situation with your new perspective and you'll always end up feeling good about it.

And what if you were one of those rare people who had a great time in high school? What if you were one of those people who dished out the abuse? I would say that you're probably unhappy now, too, right? You just can't get away with that stuff like you could back in high school, can you? Well, I hope that you have learned some lessons since you graduated and see the error of your ways. If so, you're probably wondering what you can do to make amends. Well, if you want to be happy you're going to have to do a couple of things. You need to forgive yourself for being a bully and then try to be a good person. You're not a bad person if you make an honest attempt at being good. Just keep at it and hopefully all your good deeds will outweigh the bad in the end.

The crucial thing to remember is the same for both the bullies and the bullied. Regardless of what you did or had done to you, you're not in high school anymore. Get used to it.

Let nature take its course.

When it comes to life, you just can't force things.

Have you ever tried to fit a square peg into a round hole? Well, it's pretty tough and there are some good reasons why it won't work. It's because it's just the way things work in the physical world. The same thing goes for straight lines. Nature hates straight lines. This is why we never see them except where man has had some impact.

Of course, you're probably wondering what all this nature stuff has to do with your being happy. If you think about it, it has everything to do with it. By trying to stay in control of everything, we are, in essence, trying to put a square peg into a round hole. We are trying to order our universe. We are trying to make nature draw straight lines. We are trying to live our lives not as nature dictates, but rather the way that outside forces like careers and cultural role models encourage.

Here's an example: You go on a date with a person and you have a good time. In the "new" world of emotionally detached romantic interaction, the next thing that you're supposed to do is to ignore the person and play hard to get. While this may create the want and desire in the person to pursue you further, this is not what actually causes the problems that plague people who follow this line of thinking. The problems arise because the new rules of dating dictate that you should keep this up through the remainder of the relationship. This is because the "new" point of a relationship is not to let yourself freefall into happiness, but rather to play games and maintain control in the relationship at all costs.

Or how about this:

A woman wants a child very badly. However, she has a high-powered career where she cannot possibly take time off for maternity leave. Well, it's not that she can't take the time off, because she can. It's a federal law. It's just that she won't because all her competitors (usually male) are nipping at her heels. She cannot show that she is so weak and unprofessional to allow herself the option of stepping out of the game for a while to have the child. She has to show that she is as much of a man as the men. What is her prize in all this? Stress and unhappiness over not being able to do what she really wants to do.

If we look at the example of the happiest people on earth, you will see that they do not complicate their lives in these ways. They are too busy working at trying to fulfill their basic human needs that they don't have time for all these extraneous constructs that only work to sap their happiness. They let nature take its course because they don't have a choice. They are fully human and are not trying to order their lives in any way except by finding something to eat when they are hungry, loving others when they feel like it and getting out of the weather when necessary. If we could just do this, we would be much happier. Instead, we de-emphasize our basic human needs so that we can succeed at all costs. After all, human emotions are a sign of weakness and will only get in the way of what our society deems as a prosperous, successful life. Other than money and career, anything we hold near and dear is dead weight holding us back. Our values are completely reversed and that is why so many of us lead such shallow, empty lives.

Is there any reason why we can't strip down our lives so that we can truly see what our priorities truly are? There isn't. Sure, outside forces will keep us from letting us follow our natural instincts for self-fulfillment and happiness, but that's where we need to be able to use our discerning eye to determine what is necessary to us and what is necessary to other people's opinions of us as well as what is best for society.

Being happy is simple. We just have to learn to let our human nature come first.

There is no reward in misery.

This may sound like a stupid question, but what exactly do you have to gain by being miserable? I'm not being facetious. What are you getting out of it? I'm sure it's not much.

If you can start thinking about your attitude in these terms, then it should become clear that you aren't really getting anything out of being unhappy. Seriously. Is it going to help you accomplish anything? Is it going to make you rich? Is it going to make you popular? Is it going to make you feel good? I didn't think so.

Oh wait, there is one thing that it may do. It might make people feel sorry for you. At least until they can no longer stand you, that is. But that's just about it. After you pull your *poor-poor-pitiful-me* routine a few times too many, then people won't be as generous with the sympathy chiefly because they'll start dodging you. No one wants to hang around someone who's a whiner or makes them feel guilty because they "have it better" than you. Sure, you may be able to get your way sometimes by doing this, but make no mistake, it's a very manipulative way to act around others. You can only pull this stuff for so long before people start avoiding you.

Once again, I know that this is a simplistic approach, but I have found out that people relate best to things they know. They like to get something out of their efforts. Nobody likes to intentionally waste his time and effort on something that isn't going to pan out. The same goes for being miserable. I've seen people who have been stuck in a rut for years because they just can't get over themselves. They can't see or appreciate exactly how good they have it. They can't look around and see that there are many people out there who have it far worse than they do but somehow manage to be happy. They just don't have any perspective. And as I continue to repeat throughout this book, perspective is everything. Don't take yourself so seriously that you lose sight of what is important to you.

So, the next time you start feeling yourself falling into a hole of despair and self-pity, just remember that misery is its own reward. Take a step back, analyze the situation and see if there is a reward to being miserable.

I don't think you'll find one.

Keeping your options open?

If you're like me, you notice time and time again that, according to the model presented to us by the entertainment industry, the point of dating isn't necessarily to have a relationship, but rather to have lots of dates. Keeping one's options open seems to be the primary mindset when it comes to romantic interactions with others. A person can't settle on just one person because you never know who else might be just around the corner. Now, it doesn't take a rocket scientist to figure out that this is not the natural state of things. This self-imposed emotional detachment isn't biological or normal. *"I don't want to get too close too soon."* *"I love you, but I'm not in love with you."* These sorts of phrases are representative of exactly what I'm talking about. When did it become wrong for a person to actually want to spend time with another person?

Remember dating is not like an all-you-can-eat buffet where you have to save room because you don't want to eat too much of only one thing. The point of dating should be to form a relationship, not to go through as many people as possible. If you have feelings for a person, don't doubt yourself and think that you have to push yourself away from the table. Your biology knows more than some television show about who is right for you. Love is not something that needs to be delayed. When it happens, it happens and you shouldn't put it off or force yourself to remain emotionally detached.

This sort of thinking doesn't just apply to dating. It also applies to all areas of your life where you deny yourself just to keep your options open. Whether it is where you live or your job, if you like something, allow yourself to like it. Don't sit on the fence just because you think that's it's not cool to commit.

The moral of the story is if you actually like someone you're dating, don't follow the example of people on TV shows who are only about putting notches on their bedposts. Let your heart rule and let what happens happen. This may sound like old-fashioned advice, but staying detached from that which you want will not only leave you detached, but also alone.

Don't let your family drive you crazy.

It's too bad that life isn't like the movies, isn't it? If real life were like the movies, then families would always be warm, loving groups of people who help nurture and comfort each other.

Or they would be absolutely insane.

Either of these extremes would be much easier to handle than what exists in reality because it's easier to deal with clear cut stereotypes than it is to deal with the murky dynamics that make up actual families. In real families, parents may not yell at the children out of love or stereotyped ethnic behavior, but rather because they are unhappy, miserable people. Brothers and sisters may not be close or even like each other that much. While this sometimes happens on TV, usually there is a resolution in sight. In real life, the reasons for the schism may be so vague and undecipherable that they may never be uncovered. Also, in real families, people may really love each other but do not show affection. The family dynamic is very complicated and if you let it, it will drive you crazy. It can also make you very unhappy. Especially if you believe what you see on TV.

Now, I know that it's hard, but you have to realize that when you're dealing with your family, you are not just dealing with the people who comprise it; you are also dealing with all the baggage that's accumulated through the years. Because you are closer to these people than probably anybody else around you, you know more about them and with that knowledge comes the burden of having to deal with it. With strangers, you can simply nod, smile and say, "See ya later." With family it's different and aside from estranging yourself, there aren't many options.

One thing I've noticed is that most people are both at their happiest and unhappiest when they are around their families. They are at their happiest because family get-togethers allow them the opportunity to see family they haven't seen in a while and also bring back a lot of good childhood memories. They also make people unhappy almost for the same reasons. They allow them to be around family members they don't want to see and also bring up childhood memories they would rather forget. Also, many people become unhappy when they are around their family because they think that "this time things will be better." And it usually isn't. The people who make up your family probably won't change. You need to realize this and move on with your life. Accept the conditions that exist now and hope for the best.

Another of the reasons for the unhappiness is that these people see you in a role that you have probably outgrown. If you were always "the bitchy one" to your family when you were a tween, then, even though you are now hitting forty, you will still be "the bitchy one." If your brother was the "golden child" when he was little, he is still that same "golden child" even though he just got out of rehab.

You should question these roles. Chances are they don't fit anymore (if they ever did in the first place). You don't always have to play, "the bitchy one." You don't always have to play the "scapegoat." If you can just break out of these roles, take a step back, understand the dynamic and see the situation for what it is, you will be able to negotiate any family event or holiday occasion without losing one iota of your good outlook.

Here are some keys to remaining happy around your family:

- ✓ Recognize that you will be expected to play a certain role in the family. Don't go along, but don't throw a fit either. Maintain your identity.
- ✓ Don't compare yourself to more successful relatives. They probably have a lot more problems than you think.
- ✓ Realize that these people are just your family. They may have once towered over you, but you are an adult now. Let them treat you like a kid, because you will always be a kid to them. Just don't let it get to you.
- ✓ Be glad you have a family that actually gets together. Many people don't have this.
- ✓ Stop taking yourself so seriously. Once you do this, you will be much happier.
- ✓ Don't have unrealistic expectations regarding your family's behavior. They haven't changed in the past, so what's going to make them change now?

If you want to be happy around your family, you just need to realize that the brother who always bullied you is probably going to continue to do so unless you do something about it. I'm not talking about punching him or breaking down in tears. You are just going to have to call him on it. Most adults usually cringe in family situations when you address their behavior in a context that is outside the family. For example, you have a brother who always makes fun of your clothing because you are a stylish person and he is a complete slob. Instead of accepting it because you are "the weird one" of the family, just address his fashion sense in an objective way. If he dresses like a TV preacher or smells bad, make mention of it. I know that this is not necessarily taking the high road, but if you want to overcome the situation, you are going to have to serve him up a little bit of what he's dishing out. He will most likely be speechless because he hasn't developed a script to deal with your new role. Taking his behavior to task outside the family context will throw him for a loop.

I know that being happy around your family is a lot more difficult than what is portrayed in the movies, but if you can just keep your head about you, you can pull it off. Remember being "the pissed off" one is just as much of a role as any of the other ones you can have. They're your family and you don't necessarily want to be estranged from them. This isn't healthy. Just because they don't accept everything that is you, doesn't mean that you can't be happy. If it's one person in particular that bothers you, why not say a pleasant "hello" to him/her and then avoid him/her the rest of the time you're in his/her vicinity. This is probably the best option to avoid having your visit spoiled. Your happiness comes from within and not from without. You need to accept the fact that your family is probably not going to change for the better, but that doesn't mean that you can't change your attitude regarding them. If you can objectively look at their behavior you can neutralize any unhappiness that they may cause in the future.

Just go along for the ride and you'll be all right. But remember that you don't have to play along with anything you don't feel like. Just concentrate on the good things and accept the bad things and you'll be much happier. You have to realize that you can't change other people's behavior only how you react to it. Concentrate on yourself and be thankful that you can leave whenever you feel like it.

Game playing: Everybody loses!

It doesn't matter what it is, if given the opportunity, people will never let themselves be happy. It's just ridiculous. I have never understood it, but for some reason, people think that when it comes to their relationships with other people they have to turn a natural thing into a game. It's like people think that they have to look at dating as hunting rather than what it is, a way to meet a potential mate. They also look at the workplace as not just a place to work, but rather a place to scheme, to manipulate to their own advantage, to serve up just-desserts and to even the score.

This is absolutely pathetic.

I'm sure you're thinking, "But dating is a game, man. And I'm in it to win!" or "I can't let her know how I truly feel. Then she'll be in control. She'll be wearing the pants then." Or when it comes to the workplace, "It's a jungle out there. If I don't scheme and play the game, I won't ever get ahead."

This is complete garbage that has been engineered by unhappy people just to make other people equally unhappy. You are who is in control of you. How you want to conduct yourself with other people is the difference in being happy or "winning the game."

Let's look at the idea of a game for a second. In a game, there has to be a winner and a loser. Now think of this in terms of your relationship. Do you really want there to be a winner and a loser? I know that most people want to be the winner, but what they don't realize that this subsequently puts them in a relationship with a loser. By playing games in relationships, you're making yourself date a loser! Isn't this ridiculous?

Why do people play games in relationships anyway? It's certainly not to be happy. I think that it has to do with bad lessons learned in childhood. It's all about who holds the power. It's about who's in control. These are symptomatic of a person who does not want to let himself get close to anyone or let anyone get close to him. This is no way to begin a relationship and it is no way to continue into a relationship. It not only sucks energy from the relationship but also from the players. When you're playing to win, you can never let your guard down. That's a real headache.

This is just as true in the workplace. Everybody knows the schemers. Do you actually like these people? And even if you actually like them on a personal level, can you trust them? I didn't think so. I personally know a guy who schemes so much that he can't afford to take a day off from work lest his schemes unravel. He is a nervous wreck and walks around with his stomach in knots because he is so afraid of one of his plots backfiring. No one can stand this guy. He has lost all concept of how a person should conduct himself at work because he has been embroiled in office politics for so long. He is always on and always operating. As you can tell, he leads a fairly dismal life.

And what about the people at work who always "go that extra mile?" They make you feel bad because you're not doing the same thing. In reality, however, these people are usually just pretending to "do more" because it's what they think the boss wants to see. This is a game, too. If you have too many people in one place playing this one, it can really make you hate your job. It seems that many times people in the workplace engage in this kind of behavior to hide their inadequacies. How many times have you seen a person at work who is always, "covered up" has "too much on their plate" or "just can't seem to get done?" Usually, if you hold this person up to a little closer scrutiny, you'll notice that they never really get anything done. It's just a ruse, but for some reason, it's an effective one.

I propose this to all the game players. Why not try a new game? It's called the "letting yourself be happy in a relationship" game. Or how about its companion, "I go to work to earn a living and do a good job and nothing else" game. These games are simple to play and involve the exact same rules. They are about being honest and up front with your feelings. They are about losing your ulterior motives. Sure, you may have been hurt in the past, but is there any reason to turn the incidents when someone screwed you over into life defining moments? Surely, you're not that bitter? Surely, there is some capacity for happiness in you? Maybe you may not get ahead at the office quite as swiftly, but you'll be a lot less easy to knock down when you get there. Also, you'll spare yourself an ulcer.

Sure, it may be hard to break old habits and to actually do what you feel like doing rather than trying to stay three steps ahead of everybody else, but it is possible. It just takes a little effort. You'll find when you're honest about your feelings and motivations, it may be easier to get hurt and it may take more time to get ahead, but you'll rebound far easier and with less consequence than it would if running a scheme. You will also stand on firmer ground professionally when you do make it. Most importantly, you'll feel good about yourself and that's always worthwhile.

Why not let yourself be happy? Everybody loses when you turn your relationships with other people into games. If you want to play games, why not try bowling or tennis?

Your job and the Just Rewards Syndrome.

I know that you don't want to hear this, but it's true. Your job probably won't make you happy.

Sure there are going to be some people out there who do manage find some sort of work that really makes them happy, but these people are few and far between. And even they are probably not happy with all aspects of their jobs.

You're probably thinking that I'm painting a very miserable picture, right? Well, you're wrong. Happiness in a job or career has nothing to do with the actual job itself, but rather about your attitude. If you go to your job, day in and day out, expecting some great reward other than a paycheck, you are probably going to end up a bitter person. You'll look back upon your career when they're handing you the gold watch at retirement with much regret over not doing something else with your life even though the other path that could have been taken might have eventually turned out to be equally as dreary. You do realize that the term "starving artist" exists for a reason, right?

No, the happiness doesn't come from the job, but rather from your attitude regarding your job. If you go in, do your job to the best of your ability and are able to forget it as soon as you hit the door on the way home, you will be a happy person. Realize that your job is not you. It is just a tiny fraction of the person that you are. Sure, it provides the ways and means for you to explore your other interests, but it is probably no more than that. I know that not everybody can just put their job out of their minds as soon as they leave the building, but they do need to at least compartmentalize it. Don't think of it until the occasion arises—when the phone rings or you pull into the parking lot. Life's too short to spend worrying about work.

It seems to me that many people go into the workforce with unrealistic expectations. They expect (and are encouraged by colleges and guidance counselors) to think that they will earn extravagant salaries and have fabulous lives. They are also told not to settle, to go for the gusto, to seize the day. As a result, when they get out of school and see that they are not living an extravagant life, are not making that much money, and are in effect settling for less, it makes them depressed. The fact of the matter is that ninety-nine percent of the people in the workplace have *had* to settle. Unless you're born with a silver spoon or trust fund, you'll have to work in jobs that you won't necessarily like just to eat and pay the bills. This is a fact of life that many people have a hard time dealing with. In fact, some people lose a lot of valuable years feeling horrible because of this. If you can just approach your job with realistic expectations, as just a job, you'll be far happier.

This is a practical approach, plain and simple. If you want to be happy in the work place, just let the job be a job and nothing more. It's not your identity. If you can separate yourself from it, you can stop any notion that you are being lost in it. You can also stop what I like to call the *Just Rewards Syndrome.*

The *Just Rewards Syndrome* is the notion that if we do something good, then we will inevitably be rewarded for it in a similar matter. For example, you field an important phone call that saves the company hundreds of thousands of dollars while the boss is taking one of his two-hour lunches. You probably think that you should be rewarded for it with a bonus of some kind. Of course, if you've ever worked anywhere at all, you know that this is probably not going to happen. You're probably going to get a "Thanks for taking my call" and a "Could you make some more coffee?"

While in our rational minds we know this is going to happen but in our minds that have been programmed by the notion of "just rewards", we think that we are going to get something for it. You have to realize that many companies believe that a compliment is more beneficial to an employee than a raise. While I think that this is a very self-serving and naïve attitude on the part of the corporate world, there's not really much we can do about it. So don't expect anything better and you won't develop a bad attitude over it. If you can just separate yourself from the job, you can overcome this idea of the *Just Reward*. If you can take a step back, you can get a closer look at the big picture.

But how can you do this?

The best way to do this is to periodically take a vacation that is completely unrelated to your job. This allows you time to step back and just be you. It allows you to reboot and get back to your core thinking. If this isn't possible, at least take a little time off. I would even go as far as suggesting taking a day off occasionally just to sleep in and watch some TV. You have to periodically reconnect with who you really are. And if this isn't possible, it would be good to take up a hobby. Anything that will make you get out of the rut of workplace thinking.

Once again, don't count on your job to make you happy. It won't. The only way you will be happy is if you allow yourself to be happy. Stop waiting around for something good to come along. Stop waiting around for a better job or a "just reward". Just step outside the job, get in touch with who you really are and start letting yourself be happy.

So what if people think you're a failure?

And you thought that you only had your own opinion of yourself to worry about! Throwing other people into the mix can result in more confusion and self-doubt than you ever had on your own. But it doesn't have to be this way. This kind of unhappiness is easy to overcome if you just know where it's coming from.

It's like this: When it comes to melancholia and unhappiness, nothing brings these out as much as seeing a friend, family member or rival doing better than you. It's just enough to make you stay in bed and cry. These people were your inferiors, after all! You were there when they couldn't figure out how to use the ATM. You were there when they thought that Washington DC and Washington State were the same place. It's just too much to bear.

So, how did this person get ahead of you?

Dwelling on this question will make you crazy and will fuel your unhappiness for the rest of your life if you let it. How they got ahead is not really relevant, but how you deal with the fact that you are not doing as well as someone with less talent and ability is.

Remember my tips on how to be happy? The one that applies in this case is the one about always doing everything to the best of your ability. If you do your best, then that that's all you can do. You just have to concern yourself with being the best *you* that you can be and stop worrying about how other people are doing. Maybe fortune hasn't smiled on you the way that it has on the other person. Maybe he has problems that you wouldn't ever want to have or even know about. Being successful in the eyes of society isn't always what it's cracked up to be. I have seen people who were far more successful than me have problems with paying their bills. I have seen them have problems with drugs and alcohol. I have seen people living in big houses who couldn't pay their utility bills. I have seen people with the big SUVs who couldn't afford the gas or insurance for them. They survive on credit cards because it's the only way they can keep up the appearance of being *successful.*

Being successful financially or in your career has nothing to do with being successful as a person. As long as you do what you like in your everyday life and pursue the things that make you happy, you will be doing well. You are probably already there, but just don't realize it because you've become confused. You see stuff on TV that just isn't true in real life. You see nineteen-year-old millionaires and twenty-three-year-olds marketing VP's. This isn't reality. Does anyone really want to do business with a company that makes a twenty-three-year-old into a vice president? He might have trouble scheduling board meetings around keg parties.

Seriously.

Never think of yourself as a failure. Sure, you may not have moved the world on a grand scale, but you probably have affected the lives of those around you for the better. The lessons of *It's a Wonderful Life* are true. When you help people you are creating positive memories in the minds of others. You will be the "person who helped me pick up my papers" or "that man who gave me directions." While it may not seem like something that is worthy of a prize or anything, this is still important stuff. It does have a positive impact on the world. Everybody does have a part to play in life and our job is to realize that maybe our part is not always a grand one. Sometimes it may be, but most of the time it won't. We can only do our best at everything we do even if it's as mundane as helping someone with their groceries. Once you add them up, a lot of small good deeds can be more important than one big one.

You need to realize too that even though a person is considered successful, if you were to ask them about facets of their lives other than their career or money, you would probably see that things aren't necessarily that rosy under the surface. Maybe a man is a millionaire but has never really been in love. Maybe a woman is a successful lawyer but has never had a successful relationship. Maybe a beauty queen sees herself as a fat little girl who never got invited to the dance. Maybe a successful actor is still fearful of being rejected by his fans. These are not farfetched examples. Success is largely figured by how we view ourselves. A person can be successful and still be unhappy. If you don't accept the fact that you're doing as well as you can do under the circumstances, it doesn't matter how much money you have in the bank.

Another thing to think about is that there is no magic formula to being happy. You just have to accept yourself and what you have and don't let it crush you if success doesn't come your way. Success should be viewed as something "extra", not as the end-all-be-all. If you can think like this, it'll be a lot easier to appreciate when good things do happen for you.

The objective to you not seeing yourself as failure is yourself. You should never focus on the successes of your peers because I'm sure that you will not pay as close attention to their failures. For some reason, we have a tendency to enhance the successes of others, while downplaying our own. You must overcome this tendency. We only have so much time on this earth and death is the great equalizer. No matter what you do in life, we all end up in similar circumstances. It's just that the path is a little bit different. So, my tip to you is to enjoy yourself at what you do. And if you can't enjoy your job, make an even bigger effort to enjoy your life. Life's too short to spend it comparing yourself to other people.

As long as you do your best and put forth your best effort, no one, especially not you, can look at you as a failure.

Accept the fact that some people will treat you badly.

If you're going to be happy, you're going to have to stop beating yourself up about something. It's something that all of us live with, but for some reason never truly accept or even recognize. It is something you're going to have to accept at face value. I know that this is a hard one, but not everybody out there is going to like you.

What? But this can't be!

Yes, it's true. It's a fact of life that everybody you meet is not going to think that you're the greatest person they've ever met. In fact, some people you meet may think that you are simply terrible.

You protest, "But I'm so charming!"

Not everybody is going to think so. And the sad thing about this is that there may not be any good reason for them to think this about you. Maybe you remind them of somebody they don't like. Maybe your voice annoys them. There is any number of reasons why people may not always fall in love with you. What I'm saying not only applies to your everyday activities but also to relationships. In any manner of human interaction, these same dynamics apply. No matter what you do, not everybody is going to think you're the berries or the bees-knees or anything else other than a pain in the neck.

And another thing, even if you become a very successful person, don't expect everybody to be happy for you. As you should know by now, unless, of course, you've never learned any life lessons, most people don't like to see other people do well. It's just a fact of life.

If you are going to be happy, you cannot go around expecting everybody to love and accept you. If you are doing this, it's probably because you don't accept yourself and are looking for some sort of affirmation from everyone else. This isn't healthy. Also, it puts you in a position where you are going to have to compromise yourself in order to get these people to like you. While this may make you happy in that regard for a while, you will probably eventually be unhappy because you had to do something that either you didn't want to do or didn't really believe in.

Think of it this way. Do you really want everybody to like you? I want you to turn this over in your mind. By everybody I mean *everybody*. Do you want the snobs to like you? The people who won't give you the time of day unless you're offering to humiliate yourself for them? Do you want bad people to like you? The ones who stiff the wait staff on tips and never offer to pay for drinks?

You get the picture.

People who try to get everybody to like them will usually end up with no one liking or respecting them. It's that simple. These people will appear to be phony and no one will able to discern who you really are.

I know that it's tough to come to the acceptance that not everybody is going to like you, but if it's any consolation you should realize that not everybody is going to dislike you either. It works both ways. There are going to be people out there who absolutely adore you and there won't be any good reason why. I don't know if it's chemistry or what, but some people will like you no matter what.

The funny thing about this, and you should know what I'm going to say, is that you already know this stuff. Everything I'm telling you, you already know. For some reason, you just can't seem to let it sink in. You know that you like some people more than others for no apparent reason. You also know that sometimes you don't like other people for no apparent reason. Maybe it's pheromonal or maybe it's just body language. Who knows? It's just the way it is. As I keep reiterating, I am firmly convinced that one of the main reasons people are unhappy is because we're always trying to override nature. We don't let our truly human selves rule. We're always trying to over-intellectualize everything and this is no exception.

The bottom line is this: The only people you should want to like you are the people who will like you for who you are. Not because you're acting like somebody you're not. These are the people you don't have to try so hard with. If you try to be anybody other than who you already are in order to get somebody to like you, you're just fighting a losing battle. If you are able to pull it off and curry some favor, you didn't really get anyone to like you. You only managed to get people to like the character you created. And by doing this, you probably alienated the people who liked the real you. It's a no-win situation if you try to do this. It's best not to even get started down that road. And if you're already on it, just stop. Let the chips fall where they may. You are only making yourself unhappy by pretending to be something you're not.

So, just be yourself and don't worry about it. Live your life the way you want and don't try to cater to what you think other people may or may not like. Do they make you happy? Are they going to pick you up when you're down? Probably not. Just think about that the next time you start trying to win people over. People who truly care for you will rarely let you down. Stop trying to win the favor of people who will only use you and turn a blind eye when you have a problem.

If you don't like somebody when you meet them, they probably don't like you. Your instincts are a lot better than you think if you can just stop over-intellectualizing and listen to yourself. You're better off without everybody liking you anyway.

But what if I don't know why I'm unhappy?

Now it's time for the inevitable question. "All this advice is good and all, but what if it doesn't really apply to me? What if I don't really know why I'm unhappy?"

Well, it's like this: Unhappiness is not always a clear cut thing. Sometimes, it's not so easy to figure out what it is that is dragging us down. Some people can point to a life-defining moment that changed their outlook. This is a moment that can be looked at and remembered as the time when their happiness died. It might be the death of a spouse or a child, or it could even be a time when their dreams were crushed. However, for many of us, unhappiness is like a thief in the night that sneaks up on us and takes up residence in our psyche and doesn't want to leave. This is when we start getting depressed. We can wake up feeling low and just plod around for days in an undefined funk that doesn't really make much sense. If we could just figure out what it is, then we could do something about it.

While your unhappiness may seem formless, there is definitely a method to it. I think if you really looked hard you would find it. In other words, I'm saying that you know what it is, but either are too afraid or don't want to recognize it.

Most of us start out happy in life, but as time goes by we gradually get beaten down by the bad things that happen to us. It might be a bad break-up or a failed opportunity but if we're not conscious of how we're reacting inwardly to this adversity, we can become emotional basket-cases without even knowing it. Things that we have taken for granted may come along later and trigger those feelings of unhappiness. It might be a book title or a photograph. It might be something we saw on TV. It's irrelevant what it is. The fact of the matter is that when you say that you don't know why you're unhappy, you're just lying to yourself. If you relax and free your mind and stop hiding, you'll figure it out easily enough.

I know that there are free-floating anxieties out there and some people are prone to panic attacks. However, I also know that outside of chemical imbalances, there is always a reason why you act a certain way in a certain situation. Maybe you get nervous when guys bigger than you start gesturing wildly. Maybe you're afraid of clowns. Regardless of the circumstances, this behavior didn't start by itself. Maybe you can't trace the exact origin, but you know that you act this way in certain situations. All I'm saying is that if you relax and meditate enough about it, the thing that causes this behavior will come bubbling up from that brain of yours. The same is true when it comes to unhappiness. You know, whether you want to recognize it or not, that certain things make you unhappy. And I'm willing to bet that you know why or what it is.

So, what if you still don't know why you're unhappy?

I'm not buying it. I think that you're far more capable than that. I also think that you're more self-aware than you're giving yourself credit for. The moral of the story is if you have no clue as to why you're unhappy you're either lying to yourself or you're not looking deeply enough. Most of the time I've found the answer is a lot more obvious than you think if you'll just be honest with yourself. In fact, it's usually so simple, once you figure it out, you'll wonder what the big deal is.

Don't memorialize the bad things.

All of us have a tendency to get sentimental over things. It might be an old bandana that you wore to that Guns and Roses concert back in high school or it might be an old pair of jeans that you happened to be wearing when you met your true love. It doesn't matter. We like to keep things around that make us remember the happier times. There's nothing wrong with this. It's good to have things that help us to look back fondly upon our lives. However, this same principle of *memorializing* doesn't just end there. We do the same thing with the bad things in our lives. While these memorials may not always be material things, they do loom large in our minds and can take the form of life-defining moments or grudges.

Of course, you understand that I'm not talking about completely eliminating the bad memories. This is unwise and unlikely to happen. It's good to look back on your past mistakes as lessons or trial runs. The bad things that have happened to you should be viewed as training courses in how to react the next time they happen. This kind of healthy reminiscing is not what I'm talking about. What I'm referring to is when you look at the bad stuff as the point at which your life changed for the worst.

For example, how often have you watched a TV show that has portrayed an event as a turning point in the character's life? While it's true that events can change your life, you are the person who is truly in charge of this. Don't treat every bad experience like you're a child who's just been scolded. When someone says something that's not necessarily nice to you, just let it go. Don't make it an active source of anger just waiting to be remembered and stirred up. Holding a grudge is never healthy.

Even the happiest people in the world have had bad things happen to them. Some of them have been through absolute hell on earth, yet they still remain happy. What separates them from the chronically unhappy is how they deal with it. They don't treat the bad experiences as life changing events. They look to them as "dark periods" or a "learning experiences." They know that the measure of a man is not in how he acts, it's how he reacts. The thing that separates them is that they remain their core self regardless of what happens to them. Extraneous events may enhance or temporarily affect who they are, but it doesn't change them. If you are to be happy and have a better attitude this is what you must do. Remain true to yourself and don't dwell on the bad stuff. And better yet, don't construct monuments to the bad events in your life.

Accept the fact that bad things will happen to you. This much is inevitable. We don't live in a perfect world. However, you have to keep in mind that even though bad things will happen to you, good things will happen too. There is a balance in the world and you have to make peace with it. Accept the world as is and also accept the fact that in order to understand it, you have to learn that you can't understand it. Once you realize this, you can de-emphasize the bad and move on. There's no need to memorialize unpleasant things. These memorials will only serve to block your path to happiness.

Happiness and other people. What the "experts" don't tell you.

Let's face it, in order to be happy we all feel that we need to feel accepted by other people. I know that this will be an affront to many of you so-called "independent" types. Yes, we know that you are a strong individual who doesn't need the approval of anybody. You are an island. You can do everything by yourself. And you can usually do it better than anyone else, right?

Yeah, yeah, we know…

In addition to that, we also know that many self-help gurus and psychologists always insist that it's important for us to achieve a state where we are fully-functioning, independent people free from the opinions of others. We should need no one in our lives unless we consciously choose to allow someone into the inner sanctum that is us.

If this is the case, why are we always trying to make a connection with other people? Why do we get married if we're so self-sufficient and independent? Why do we have kids who will love us unconditionally? And this one is for the TV self-help gurus. If needing people is so bad, then why are they asking us to keep tuning in to their shows? If these people are practicing what they preach, then they should be telling us that there's no need for us to watch them!

Of course, the answer to this one is obvious. We all seek the approval of other humans. We seek that that connection with other people. It's in our biology. We are social creatures. Some of us are more social than others, but regardless, we do seek that support. This is okay. It's just part of our human nature. But when our desire to seek approval turns us into cringing, simpering fools who will do anything to get people to like us, then we have a problem.

To avoid this, you have to maintain a balance and to realize that while you need the love and affection of other people, you cannot expect them to make you happy. They can help to enhance your happiness, but you can't depend on them for your happiness. Your happiness has to come from within.

It's like this. You can't expect someone to carry you up the mountain. You have to climb it yourself. You are your own person and are the sum of your own parts. Sure, that crazy guy you met in college may make you laugh, and your girlfriend may make you feel absolutely wonderful, but if you aren't happy within, these people probably aren't going to want to have anything to do with you. Unhappy people who depend on other people to make them happy only succeed in sucking the energy out of all those around them.

You don't want to be that kind of person, do you? I hope not anyway.

One tip to being happy around other people is to surround yourself with upbeat individuals with good attitudes. When you're around good people, it's amazing how easily your happiness comes out. This will allow the true you to emerge, the one that doesn't depend on others to make him happy. The one that can be happy by himself, but is such a great guy that other people want him around as well.

And what if you can't find any upbeat people to be around?

Sadly enough, this is going to be the case sometimes. When this happens, don't doubt yourself or your personality. You need to ask yourself: Do you really want to be around people who bring you down? I would hope not. While it's true that you can be a good example to the downtrodden, you also have to realize that all that negative energy will probably just end up bringing you down in the process. For your sake, if you only have the option of being around negative people, maybe you should just spend your time reading a book instead.

Once again, it's human to need people. The question is which people do we need? We need happy people, but not to make us happy. We only need them to enhance the happiness we already have.

But what if I'm a hopelessly miserable person?

So, you're hopelessly miserable?

I don't think so. If you bought this book, then there's a pretty good chance that you are longing for something better. If you can recognize that you can be a happier person, then you are, by no means, a hopelessly miserable person. Maybe you're a happy person who has just somehow lost his way. Maybe some bad things have happened to you and made you doubt yourself to such an extent that you've started doubting everything. Maybe you just don't know what's good anymore. Regardless, there is hope for everyone and if you're reading this book, then there's hope for you. You know that you can do better. This should make you feel better already.

Now, I'm not saying that there aren't miserable people out there. No, I'm not saying that at all. Some people are extremely miserable. You've seen them. They're the ones who shoot down every plan or idea that sounds remotely original or fun. They're the ones who always look for the cloud behind every silver lining. Yeah, you know these people. They ooze gloom and make everybody around them feel bad. But are they hopeless? No. Nobody is hopeless.

The sad thing about it is that most of these people don't even realize what they're doing. I knew one guy who was probably the most negative person I have ever met. According to him, nothing was good. Everything was terrible. Somebody could have walked in and handed him a million dollars and he still would have found something to grumble about. However, he was clueless about how negative and miserable he was. He told me how his wife had complained about his negativity and he didn't really understand what she was talking about. I agreed with her, but I didn't say anything. I just didn't understand him. But then one day, he said something that made everything click into place. I finally understood why he was the way he was. He started talking about his father who also happened to be minister. He said that his father was the most negative person he had ever known. He said that he never had a good word to say about anything. Everything was open to his criticism, regardless of what it was. In other words, like father like son. The son was emulating the father without even realizing what he was doing. In his case, his misery was learned. I bet if the guy had just realized what he was doing, he probably wouldn't have been nearly so negative about everything. I bet he probably wasn't even really that miserable. The way he acted was just the way that he had learned to communicate.

I think that this is true of a lot of people. Children who grow up around negative parents will probably manifest a lot of those negative behaviors whether they really feel them or not. There's a lot of hope for these people. The only thing is that they have to realize how they're coming off to those around them.

The thing to remember is that you may be extremely miserable now, but you will pull out of it if you will just stop taking yourself so seriously and start enjoying life. Life's too short to be miserable and there's a whole world out there for you to enjoy. So what if things don't go your way? Nothing works out all the time for everybody. You just need to realize that you are not hopelessly miserable. No one is hopeless as long as he is doing their best. Misery can be overcome. As I keep saying, you just have to allow yourself to get out of the way and invite that happiness in.

Troubling thoughts.

As if you didn't have enough to worry about with other people, a lot of the time your biggest critic is you.

Here's why: Everybody has inner dialogue. Whether it's a running monologue or an internal conversation, we are all in constant communication with ourselves. Sometimes, we have to be careful not to let this inner dialogue accidentally come out of our mouths especially when we're in less than ideal situations. Just imagine if you were at work and you let the boss know how you really felt!

However, while most of our inner dialogue is innocuous, sometimes we can be troubled by thoughts that are not necessarily good for our psyches. Mixed in with the running monologue can be thoughts that make us doubt ourselves to our very core. "Am I wasting my life?" "Have I done the best by my family?" "I should have paid more attention in school." These thoughts can ruin you if you let them. Not only that, they can put your life on hold. Just like anything else, unhappiness can become an obsession and these thoughts only serve to make this possible.

But how can you stop them? You just have to realize that the past is the past and you can't change it. I'm sure that you're going to say that this is easier said than done. However, if you really want to change, you can do it. You can't keep kicking yourself for your past mistakes. You can only do better in the here-and-now as well as in the future. You have to realize that you don't live in the past or the future. You live in the present and that's why you have to make sure that you do your best in the now. There may even be some truth to your inner troubling thoughts, but you can't let that stop you. You probably did the best you could under the circumstances. It's like the old saying about crying over spilled milk. The same goes with your life.

You ask, "But what if I really know that I could be doing better with my life?" and "But what if I feel like a loser whenever I'm around my friends?" My answer is that you're going to have to accept the fact that you are only as successful as you are right now. Sure, you may not have done as well as you would have liked, but as long as you're doing the best you can, you're going to be okay. There's always room for improvement, right? While you may have fiddled around in the past and wasted time, that part of your life is over. You just have to pledge to do better and you'll be surprised how those troubling thoughts will disappear.

Regret over our lives is a big part of why we are unhappy, but it is fixable. You can get over it, if you'll just realize that there's really nothing you can do about the past. Nobody can be proud of everything they've done. Obsessing over what you may have done wrong or how you might have done better is going to get you nowhere. Unhappiness is one of the biggest obsessions that any of us can have, but if we can go to sleep at night knowing that we put our all in the things that we feel are important, there will be no place for it in our lives.

Misery loves company.

If you want to remain truly unhappy, then I'm sure that you're not going to have to look hard to find someone to help you stay at the bottom. This is because, as we all well know, misery loves company.

It's true isn't it? When we're feeling bad we always want someone to commiserate with us. We want a partner in misery so that we can sit around and feel sorrowful together. This just doesn't apply to us. It also applies to other people. Just think of all the times you've been in a good mood and some miserable acquaintance has come along and started telling you all his problems. This probably caused you to join him in his gloomy frame of mind, didn't it?

Even when we're not feeling bad, there are many people who would like us to join them in their misery. And most of the time, they get us to join in whether we want to or not. Being around negative people can make a person be negative, even if that's not even his natural inclination.

Remember that unhappiness and misery are just like drugs. Just like it isn't good for recovering addicts to hang around drug users, the same goes for hanging around miserable people. If you're trying to be a happy person and are on your way to accepting yourself and getting into a good frame of mind, then the last thing you need is to hang around unhappy people. All it takes is for one miserable person to come up to you and start talking about how she can't pay her bills this month and how her husband is cheating on her or whatever and soon you're sympathizing. The next thing you know, you're starting to magnify and dwell on all the bad things in your life. You can't help but start shifting the emphasis in your life from the good things to the bad things. And if you don't quite go this far, you will at least start feeling guilty because you don't have the problems that these people have. It's a no win situation.

So, how can you remedy this situation? The best thing to do is to avoid these miserable people as much as you can. I know that this isn't always possible because sometimes you may work with or even be related to them. In this case, whenever they start going on with the negative details of their miserable lives, just try to smile, nod and detach. Just let it go in one ear and out the other. If you can't do this, offer logical tips on what they can do to change their situations. Chances are they won't like what you have to say or will completely ignore you. However, at least, you will have done something to help and you haven't done anything to feed their misery. You just have to not get sucked into their misery. I know that this may sound a little cold and unsympathetic, but how else are you going to protect your mental well-being? Face it, if you're wallowing in misery with these people, how are you going to have a good attitude about your own life?

Misery does indeed love company and you won't have to look hard to find someone to feel miserable with you. My advice is that you need to try to avoid miserable people and surround yourself with positive individuals, people with good attitudes who aren't always down and dejected. It's good to sympathize and empathize with people who are less fortunate than you, but you have your own mental well-being to take care of. Helping people is good, but what help are you going to be if you're just as down as them? You've got enough problems without taking on everybody else's.

Stop doubting yourself.

You probably know more about yourself than you do about any other person in the world, right? I would hope so, anyway. This is true of all of us. We constantly think about ourselves. We have inner dialogues where we solve our problems. We rehearse our inner scripts to cope with the world. We think about our childhood and our families. We think about our school days and our hopes and dreams. We are the center of our universe and we can't help it. We are the greatest role we will ever play. We should have PhD's in the study of ourselves.

Now here's the funny thing: If we know more than anyone else about ourselves, then why is it that we are constantly doubting ourselves and making ourselves unhappy? We usually know what's best for us, but we will let any Tom, Dick or Harry come along and tell us otherwise. We also know when we are good at something and when we are talented. However, we let people who know nothing about us put us down and tell us that we can't do things when we know otherwise. We actually act as though they know more about us than we do. This is absurd! This causes us to think that every move we make is wrong and that we can't possibly be right about anything. Negative thoughts about our abilities hinder our day to day interactions with others and interfere with our happiness.

The problem lies not just in our self-doubt, but also in our confidence. While we subconsciously know that we are the authority on us, we have a tendency to think that others may "know something" that we don't. As social creatures, we seek the approval of others. This is natural, but this desire for acceptance sometimes can tendency to carry over into other areas, ones that can open us up to subtle personal attacks on our abilities or self-confidence. The thing to realize is that most of the time, these personal attacks are perpetrated not because of something that you have done, but because of the perpetrator's personal motivation. He may feel threatened because you're a better tennis player than him so he'll start trying to either "help" you with your game by giving you bad advice or start "trivializing" your ability. It's hard to believe, but not everyone has our best interests at heart. Jealousy is a very real thing and can make even your closest allies sabotage you. It's a hard pill to swallow, but, for the most part, people do not want to see you succeed. They think if you do well, then they look bad. This shouldn't depress you. It should open your eyes and make you realize that you have to try harder and don't be upset when your "friends" don't necessarily support you. Protect your self-confidence and don't let others undermine it.

I'm not saying that we should ignore all criticism. There are occasions where the truth will hurt, but it's usually easy to see this. In order to judge if a person's criticism is genuine, just look at the person.

Ask yourself the following questions:
- Is this person a rival?
- Does this person's criticism make sense?
- Is this person mean-spirited?
- What does this person have to gain by telling me this?

If you follow these guidelines, it should be fairly easy to determine the motivation of a person's criticism. You can see if it's genuine or just a mean-spirited person's attempts to make you doubt yourself. These are the types that aren't engaging in constructive criticism. They are *putting you down.* Even though it may hurt, some people in life will have good reasons to criticize you and will be correct in doing so. Most likely, whether you know it at the time, you will eventually recognize the truth in their words if they're sincere.

Self-doubt can be a big factor in your unhappiness. Just how can you be confident and secure if you think that every movement you make is a potential fatal error or misstep? As I keep reminding you throughout the book, the important thing is to always do your best so you don't have to worry about what you're doing or what you did wrong all the time. It's true that you will make mistakes, but sometimes there will be no way they can be avoided. You cannot let them hold you down. Look at them as learning experiences and you'll grow stronger and your confidence will become more secure. I have made quite a few mistakes in my life, some of which still make me cringe. However, I have tried to learn something from each one so that I did not repeat it again. It would be wonderful if we lived in an idyllic world where nothing went wrong and everybody was on our side. We would be free from doubt and there would be no one to make us think otherwise. However, with this kind of naiveté, we would be easy pickings if the wrong person came along. We must strengthen ourselves against self-doubt and the people who want to tear us down.

Self-doubt can ruin you. It can make you unhappy and lead to you making others unhappy if you don't watch it. If you can just remember that you are the expert on you, it'll be easy to start building your self-confidence. You know yourself and your abilities. You know when you are learning and growing. You know when you are good at something. Don't let others take that away and make you feel bad about yourself. Unhappiness is just a symptom of a lot of other problems in your life. Self-confidence is the answer to eliminating a lot of them.

Your friends.

Everybody says that friends are a source of happiness. This may be true some of the time, but if you're like most people, you've found that your friends can also make you miserable. We've all heard the song telling us what friends are for, but what we didn't hear is about how we're more likely to betrayed by our so-called friends than by people we don't even know.

Of course, this makes perfect sense because perfect strangers have no need to do harm to you. They simply don't care. But your so-called friends may have been harboring resentment towards you since the day you met. Maybe you insulted them by not saying hello in the way they like. Maybe you didn't remember their birthday. Maybe they're jealous. Regardless, don't take it for granted that your friends will always do their best by you.

This is a pretty bleak picture, isn't it? A dark world where your friends are not who they seem can be a dangerous place. We're taught from childhood that friends are everything and this is true at the time. However, is it any coincidence that when you get older, your parents start making rude comments about the people you hang out with? It's because they know more than you at the time about how fickle friendships can be. They have been down this road before and know all too well that that fella who's slapping you on the back and laughing at all your jokes may be secretly plotting to steal your girlfriend.

It's enough to make a person paranoid. But it doesn't have to be. I realize that you know exactly what I'm going to say about this, but I'm going to say it anyway. You just have to accept that this is nature of adult human dynamics. As people get older, they get more desperate. Their needs change. I know this from personal experience. I have been burned in more friendships than most people. However, I took a long hard look at myself and realized what my problem was. I hadn't matured to the point of adult friendship. Honorably and naively too, I must add, I viewed friendship as I had viewed it in my school days. Subsequently, I was a target of people who sought to take advantage of me or worse, do me harm. I was never terribly hurt by these episodes, but I was somewhat puzzled. I usually went out of my way to be a good friend and was always ultimately treated with disrespect. However, after a while, I finally figured it out. It was a hard truth, but I am far happier now than I was when I was without a clue.

The thing is that you shouldn't be upset if people you thought were your friends turn out to be anything other than that. This is perfectly normal and it's probably not your fault. People will turn on you for a variety of reasons.

I don't know why the friendship dynamic changes as you get older. It seems as a person ages, his/her priorities change. A person moves closer to his/her spouse or children (hopefully) and considers other relationships less important. I think that this shift in allegiances is sometimes a little heavy handed and leaves some people with somewhat of a cutthroat mentality. They say, "What the hell. I'm not married to this person. I don't owe them anything. I can screw them over as much as I want!" This warping of perspective is the reason why some people just aren't friend-material. They just don't understand the dynamic anymore.

Perhaps, it's because they never matured past the high school camaraderie phase. I don't know, it could be any number of things. What they may not have done to their friends only ten years earlier in their lives now seems like the only option. If your friend's getting ahead means betraying your trust, don't be surprised if you're the one on the losing end.

The main thing to understand is that even though some of your so-called friends may try to screw you over, you cannot become a hermit. You still have to get out there and make friends because it's part of who you are. Just keep the big picture in mind. People are people and will act accordingly. Choose your friends wisely and if they stab you in the back, just chalk it up to experience and realize that they weren't worth having as a friend anyway. Don't blame yourself and let the experience turn you into a miserable person.

Don't be a know-it-all.

In my opinion and as I have said over and over again, the biggest obstacle people have in living happy, fulfilled lives is none other than themselves. I know I'm certainly my biggest roadblock and I don't think I'm that much different from anybody else.

One of the things that blocks our way to happiness is the fact that we think we know it all. About everything. I know that there are some of us who have the fake humility and assumed zero self-confidence. But let's be realistic, even these people can sometimes look at the world through such a narrow, egocentric view that they cannot possibly see a true picture of what's going on around them. This includes their home life, their interactions with others and their overall general demeanor.

You've heard of people who can't see the forest for the trees. This is exactly what I'm talking about. They know themselves so well that they lose track of how they are actually coming off to the world. They become so embroiled in their inner dialogue that their self-image somehow gets disconnected from reality. A person may think that he's a clever, outgoing guy, but in reality he's a sadistic bully. He just doesn't have a clue.

I know that this is probably your next question: "But I thought you said that we are the experts when it comes to knowing ourselves?" Well, this is true. However, if you'll remember I also said that some criticism is warranted. It's the motive behind the criticism that's important to discern. Also, since you are the expert on yourself, you'll need to learn when your self-image may be slightly off-kilter with what's really going on. We all have a lot to learn and we'll never even come close to knowing everything, but you have to make the attempt. If you close yourself off to learning anything new about yourself, you'll never make much progress.

Self-awareness is a very important part of being happy and you can't have it if you are a know-it-all. For example, I know a woman who thinks that she's the most fun-loving individual in the world. She thinks she's outgoing and witty. However, in reality she's very reserved and sort of weird acting. She's also quite withdrawn most of the time. The thing about it is that if anyone were to speak to her about how strangely she acts around others, she would probably never speak to that person again. She is so ego driven that the very idea that someone would dare tell her something that doesn't jive with how she views herself, would simply unnerve her.

The moral of the story is to open yourself to the fact that the way you view yourself might not necessarily be the way that you actually are. Sure, you may think that you're a devil-may-care scoundrel, but are you really? If you can just accept the fact that even though you know yourself better than you anybody else does and that you still have lots more to learn, you'll be much better off. You'll be able to improve the areas that need improvement and utilize your strong points. After all, how can you possibly hope to be happy if you don't even know what makes you happy in the first place?

Everybody has been mistreated. You're no exception.

Did you have a rough day? Feeling a little sorry for yourself? Was somebody mean to you?

Oh, I know. We all feel this way. This is not the problem. The problem lies in when you let these feelings linger. When you feel sorry for yourself for a prolonged period of time, you're looking at one pathetic life. No one will want to hang out with you. You won't want to do anything. You'll just be a generally miserable person. And extremely boring.

Everybody has been mistreated. Everybody feels sorry for himself sometimes. If you can understand this, then you'll see that whatever somebody did to hurt your feelings probably wasn't anything that you can't handle. It's all been done before.

But you still feel bad, right? You just want to sulk? Well, let me point something out for you that you probably hadn't thought about. If someone mistreats you, it was probably his intention for you to tuck your tail and cry all the way home. If you sit at home bawling, he will have gotten what he wanted. You're not making him feel bad by showing how hurt you are. You're showing him that you're vulnerable and an easier target than he previously thought.

You can see how this can lead to an endless cycle of unhappiness and victimization.

There are times when you are really hurt and that you really feel bad. But even then, if you milk it for all it's worth, people's sympathy will go south fast. Think about it. How would you feel about a person who refuses to get over some worthless guy who dumped her? You would probably find her extremely pathetic, right? And what about the guy who got cheated on and dumped by his long-term girlfriend? He still carries a torch to this day. He hasn't moved on with his life. He hears her name and he gets misty-eyed. He smells her perfume and he has to go to the bathroom and cry. Do you really want to be this person? Do you want to be the person that the office bully can turn to mush with one insensitive comment?

Shrug it off and keep moving. You're much stronger than you think. Just keep doing what you do even though you want to cry inside. You'll get over it. It's true that it's hard to hit a moving target. Whenever somebody mistreats you, shake it off and keep going. Staying busy is one of the best cures for heartache and heartbreak. Time is the great healer and if you have a distraction, then it can work its magic. And also remember that everybody gets mistreated sometimes. It's how you handle it that matters.

Get over it!

If you learn anything from this book, be sure to learn this: Regardless of what you've done, what you'll do, what you hope to do, or what's been holding you back, you're going to have to get over these stumbling blocks if you want to be happy.

Yeah. It's that simple.

If you're going to be a well-adjusted person, you're going to have to move forward. You can't hit the pause button to bring your life to a standstill while you take time to sort out your problems. Time marches on and if you don't stay in step, you're going to wake up in a few years and wonder just what you've been doing with your life.

You're also going to have to realize that you're much bigger than your problems. You are the person who's in the driver's seat. Sure, your options may be limited, but you have to realize that you're the person who's most likely keeping you in a state of unhappiness. But what if you're in an unhappy relationship? But what if your spouse is making you miserable? Leave. If you don't, then you don't have any reason to complain. Don't leave yourself at the mercy of others. Unhappiness, as I have noted, comes from feelings of helplessness. Eliminate those and you're home free.

Whenever you're in a bad situation, just take a step aside and realize that you are indeed larger than the situation. This isn't the end of the world and there is always a solution. Maybe the solution is for you to leave the situation. Maybe the solution is for you to take charge. Maybe the solution is for you go in deeper. It's always you. Even if it's a selfless act, it's you who took action.

You're much stronger than you think you are.

Everybody suffers from feelings of inadequacy. Even the cockiest, most self-assured person out there sometimes doesn't feel up to snuff. The difference is that with these people, the feelings are only temporary. They know that the bad things will soon pass and that the tide will turn in their favor. If you can just get it into your head that the world is in a balanced state where both good and bad happen, then you can see that there's no need to be helpless. Then you can get out of the way of your happiness. You can get over whatever it is that you're hung up on and be the happy person that you so much want to be. You can get over that lost love. You can get over the feeling that you've frittered your life away. What's done is done and you need to stop living in the past. Live in the now and plan for the future. Note that I'm saying to plan for the future, not live in it. Delayed gratification is one of the worst things that you can ever fall victim to.

To get over what is holding you back, make sure that you do the following:

- ✓ Make peace with the past.
- ✓ Live in the now.
- ✓ Plan for the future.
- ✓ Have a good time regardless of how your life goes.

If this doesn't make sense to you, just give it a try. It will. In order for you to be happy now, you have to make peace with your past. You have to move on to a brighter today. Next you have to live in *the now*. Don't put off any potential happiness today for something "better" that may happen tomorrow. Don't always second guess yourself about what's good for you. Just do what feels good in regards to your mental being now and let any problems work themselves out. Plan for the future. Try to make sure that the choices you make contribute to a happy future. Don't put yourself in debt for something now that may cost you some serious interest in the future. In other words, don't get involved in what you know is a bad relationship now, in hopes that it will work out later. Instead, involve yourself in healthy pursuits so that they may grow into something even better in the future. And lastly, make you sure you have a good time regardless of how your life turns out. Just think about people you see on TV and also in your everyday life. What kind of people do you want to associate with? Those who whine and complain and are generally miserable regardless of what happens to them? Or those people who keep a stiff upper lip and always seem to bounce back with a smile wherever fate takes them? Birds of a feather flock together for a reason, you know?

Remember we're all going to end up in the same place in the end so make the most of it while you're here.

As you continue to read this book, realize that regardless of what has happened to you in life, you're just going to have to get over it, if you want to be happy. The source of your unhappiness may be something absolutely horrifying, but you're still going to have to move past it if you want to progress. It's the one thing that you absolutely have to do if you want to be happy.

Nostalgia and old friends.

When many of us reflect upon our younger years, we usually recall the friendships we had with fondness. You had such good times back then. You were so happy. Then you look at our current situations and wonder just what happened to those friends. In contrast to back then, you are relatively alone now.

What happened? Was it something you did?

Frankly, in a way yes, it is something you did. You grew up. So did your friends. That's pretty much it. When you were young and in school, you had loads of time to make friends. You had plenty of time to socialize. It's what you were supposed to do. However, if you'll remember, as you got older, your priorities changed. Your life was on its way and you didn't have time to hang out as much. Sure, you probably tried, but it eventually became almost impossible. You may have gotten married, had children or a stressful career. You may have moved away. Pretty soon, you were spending almost no time with the old gang. It happens to everybody. But you don't have to be unhappy about it. It was a different time and you were a different person. The thing to remember is that *the you* of then had a good time with your friends. At least good enough to look back with fondness.

It's very easy to become unhappy when we compare ourselves of now with ourselves of then. We were popular. We always had something going on with our friends. But before you get all misty-eyed about the good old days, you have to remember that you're probably only remembering the good stuff. This is fine, but don't start beating yourself up over your current situation because you feel you have lost something special.

So, when you're starting to feel a little melancholy about how you don't see the old gang that much anymore—don't. That was a time for goofing off and for hanging out. That was a time to form those childhood memories. Besides, you have to realize that your life hasn't come to a stop. You still can form new friendships and have good times. They may not be the same as those you had when you were a carefree teenager, but they can be just as good. It's up to you.

Surely you don't want to keep living in the past, do you?

Entitled to a good life?

I'm sure that I'm no different from anyone else out there when it comes to my childhood expectations. I watched the same TV shows and movies as you did. I saw what sorts of lives people were leading on TV and figured that my life was going to be just like that. I was going to have adventures and a good life. In fact, I just didn't think I was going to do these things, I thought I was entitled to them. I thought that everybody lived like that.

I'm also sure that you're just like me and found out the truth. Nobody is entitled to a good life.

Oh, you didn't know this? Well, I'm sorry but…

Yes, we're all alike. We all think that we're entitled to a good life and we're miserable when our expectations aren't met. This is the problem. Now, I'm not saying that we shouldn't have a good life and I'm not saying that you shouldn't work to achieve a good life. I'm just saying that you're not entitled to one. You have to work for it. Remember these famous words, "life, love and the pursuit of happiness?" Note that it says *pursuit of happiness*, not the entitlement of happiness.

Of course this notion of entitlement falls into almost every cliché of unhappiness out there. It involves the people who delay gratification because they feel if they deny themselves now, then they'll get it later. It includes people who are miserable because their lives don't match up with what they see on TV. It also involves the people who think that they don't deserve anything better because they're worthless compared to other people. And don't forget the people who think that everybody else is entitled to a good life but them. You name it, it involves you.

So, what can you do to fix the problem?

First of all, understand that you can have a good life if you work for it. Another important thing to know is that you may have to adjust your definition of a good life. If you're thinking a mansion in Beverly Hills is the only kind of good life there is, then you are sorely mistaken. A good life is in the eye of the beholder and no matter what kind of life you have, if you don't have the presence of mind to be able to appreciate the wonderful things that you do have, you will never have one. Are you healthy? Do you have a beautiful wife? A good husband? Happy kids? A place to live? These are the things that make up a good life. You just have to know that they don't just happen by themselves. You have to work for them. You also have to work to keep them. And I'm not just talking about physical labor here, I'm also referring to your mental attitude. You have to keep a positive attitude if you want to be able to appreciate the life you have.

So, are you entitled to a good life? No. But can you have one?

Yes, you can have a good life, but you have to work for it. And the funny thing about it is that once you start appreciating the things that you do have, you'll find that a good life is not all that hard to attain.

The grass is always greener.

As has already been discussed, we are truly social animals. We have to interact with others. We seek the approval of others and we just enjoy being around other people. However, that's not the only thing we do in regards to our interactions with other people. We also compare ourselves to them. And we usually end up feeling bad about it.

Since this is something that we naturally do, it's going to be a hard habit to break. In fact, it will probably be almost impossible. However, if you're going to be happy, you at least need to make an effort to stop. And if you're not able to stop, at least be able to recognize what you're doing and stop it temporarily.

Because you can't compare yourself to other people and be happy.

The reason for this is simple. If you're in a bad frame of mind, you will compare yourself to others and you will never see their flaws. All you will ever notice about other people is that they always have it better than you. They will be smarter, richer, taller and better looking. At least this is how you will perceive them. Also, and this shouldn't be a surprise, you will notice that they are happier than you. Of course, there will be days when you look at others and feel superior, but ironically if you're an unhappy person, this will just make you feel guilty. It's a no win situation. However, you can make an effort. And I guarantee that you'll be better person for it.

Comparing yourself to others can also lead to a lot of other problems. People get themselves in debt (especially with credit cards) because they look around and see that someone else has a bigger stereo or a bigger TV. Of course, the person also fails to see that there's no way that the other person can afford the stuff he has without being hopelessly in debt. And after you're in debt, that's just one more thing to be unhappy about.

One thing that really disturbs me is when people try to compare themselves to celebrities. This is one of the most destructive behaviors that you can ever engage in. The lives of famous people are foisted upon us. We see them with their fancy cars and mansions. We hear about their fabulous lives. We also see that ours pale in comparison and it can make us feel bad about ourselves. It makes us go in debt for "McMansions" and cars that we can't afford. We're still not looking the part, but we sure are trying. We're also overextending ourselves past the point of no return. We are making ourselves miserable just trying to keep up with the celebrities. Sure, it's interesting to see "what they're going to do next," but what the media doesn't focus on is all the problems that happen because of all their money, fame and success. We don't hear about their fears of being kidnapped or their lack of privacy. We don't see what they have to do behind the scenes just to get in the position to be famous. If all this stuff was as overexposed as the celebrities themselves, then I don't think we would feel quite as bad when get up for work in the morning.

So, when you start comparing yourself to others, make an effort to stop. And if you can't stop, at least recognize what you're doing and the ramifications thereof. If you must look at others, do so with open eyes. Sure, it's good to appreciate that other people have nice things, just don't filter out the bad stuff that goes along with it. You'll be a lot more appreciative of what you do have if you can look at the world objectively.

Should you rationalize your world?

Everybody has a tendency to look at their life as a story. In fact, this is what it is. A story. It has a beginning, middle and end. It's probably pretty interesting, too. At least to us, anyway. As a result of us viewing our lives in such a manner, we also try to figure out why that such and such plot point developed. Or why did this particular character develop in a particular way. I know that when I put it in this way, it sounds a little ridiculous, but we all do it. We view our lives as though we're watching a movie and try to rationalize what exactly is happening and has happened to us. We try to figure out why we took a particular step in a particular direction. We think back on why we didn't take a particular job, why we didn't pursue a particular relationship and on and on. Most importantly we wonder how we ended up at this particular place in the story.

Is this a healthy way of looking at things?

I'll tell you that it might as well be because we're certainly not going to change. Seriously though, I think that overall there's nothing wrong with trying to rationalize our lives. In fact, introspection and self-awareness are good things in that they help us to take a step back and get a reading on who we are and what we want. The only problem that occurs with rationalizing your world is when you start thinking about all the things you've done right or wrong and start second guessing yourself to a point where you come to a complete standstill. I've seen it time and time again. In fact, I've got a friend who will try to rationalize his opinion on things like movies and books to such an extent that after a while, he completely loses perspective on what he really thinks. He becomes stuck and renders himself unable to even have an opinion.

This same thing happens in a lot of people's lives. They want to always make the right move. Well, this is impossible. All you can do is your best and if you want to be happy, you should never become bogged down in your introspection because you'll never be able to appreciate or participate in what you have. The world is a crazy mixed up place that we will never be able to understand. So, face the facts and start living. Remember it's always good to look inward, just don't forget to look outward as well.

So, should you rationalize your world?

Sure, just don't think that you're ever going to completely figure it out. When you find yourself becoming unhappy and stuck, just loosen up and do what you feel makes you feel good.

Don't look to other people for the answers.

If there's one thing I've discovered to be true over the years, it's the fact that you can't look to other people for answers. The proverbial wise man who knows all is just that—proverbial. The thing you have to realize is that when it comes to answering questions regarding your life and happiness, there's only one person who can do this and that person is you.

See, you're already a lot smarter than you thought. But we've already established that earlier in the book. You are truly an expert when it comes to the subject of you.

But you're probably wondering if we already know the answers, why do we keep asking the same questions?

It's simple. The reason why you aren't able to achieve satisfaction with your life questions is because you either aren't happy with or you aren't confident enough to recognize the answer. When it comes to questions regarding the direction your life is taking or what you should do to be happy, you have to go with your gut. If you just think about what you should do and don't overanalyze, it's fairly easy to know what is the best path. All we're looking for from a "wise man" is reassurance. It's a concept that has fueled our psyches for years. "If there was only a person who knew everything..." Everybody likes to be told what to do. The important thing is that you have to be the one giving the instructions.

Something to take into consideration is that when people are first approached by cults, one of the first things they notice is that the cult members usually have all the answers to their life questions. They are confident and provide no ambiguity in their responses. It's very tempting and very natural to want to let someone else do our thinking for us. We can't let this happen otherwise we can potentially spend all our lives in a state of disillusionment. If it's really reassurance or advice you seek, simply ask for it from a parent or close family member. As for self-help gurus, it's always been fairly clear that whenever they strike a strong chord with me, it's usually when they tell me something I already know to be true. Not obviously true statements like the sky is blue or the grass is green, but rather statements like how *you can't hide from yourself* or a *don't cry over spilt milk* etc…

Unfortunately, life is not always that hackneyed. The answer is usually not just a cliché away. However, it is already within you. You usually know what it will take to make you happy if you'll just trust your instincts. We get so confused by outside influences that we sometimes forget what it is that's really bothering us. That's why we always seek help. Well, look no further than the mirror for your wise man. While you can go to others for advice, only you can figure out the answers to your life questions.

You can't control your life.

It's true. You can't control your life. But you lament, "But everyone else says that I have to be in control of my life!" You're also probably saying, "But everyone else says that I'm my own boss and that only I can make my decisions."

Yes, I agree with this. But as far as being in control goes, you're not. You can be the one driving the big bus that is your life, but you're never going to be completely in control of it. However, you can learn how to control yourself when life slaps you in the face.

Let me explain. Let's say that you're on your way to work and you leave in plenty of time, but there's an accident that blocks traffic and you're stuck for over two hours. This means you're late for work. This means that you might be fired. Were you in control of that? I think you know where I'm going with this.

However you are in control of what you do after you're fired. Do you freak out and start crying? I hope not. Do you burn bridges with your former co-workers? I hope not either. But you can conduct yourself with dignity and make it obvious to everyone that maybe they made a mistake in letting you go.

As I've said before, the primary reason why people are unhappy is because they feel that they do not have any control in their lives. They feel helpless. You have to remember that you're never helpless and while you're not in control of extraneous events in your life, you are in control of yourself. This is the answer. Once again, let me emphasize that if you can understand this, you'll be alright. Sure, you may look back ten years from now and say that you might have done better, but as long as you did your best at the time, everything will be okay.

So, remember all you can control is yourself. Your life is just the ever-changing scenario that you play off.

Guilt is an albatross.

You're miserable, right? You feel absolutely awful, right? Why?

It's because you're an absolutely awful person who isn't worthy of being happy, right? You've done something so horrible that you can never forgive yourself. You've cheated, lied or stolen. Or worse. You've been just terrible.

This all may be true. I don't know. You may be an awful person. You may have stolen your best friend's boyfriend. You may not have been there for your parents the way that you should have. You may not have been a good parent. Regardless, what's done is done and you're going to have to stop letting your guilt keep you from moving on into something better. You can't go back and change things, but you can change your future. You can take a different path than the one you're currently on.

Your guilt should not be a burden but rather a tool to help you not make the same mistakes. You feel bad about what you did and regardless of what you did, you can't go back and un-do it. You can only try to do better in the future.

It may be that you didn't even do anything really that bad, but because of manipulative parents, you just feel unworthy and guilty all the time. Some parents see guilt as an easy way of making their children behave. Sure, it may instill a good moral compass in the child, but if the parents are overzealous in their efforts, sometimes the child can feel bad when they do just about anything, whether it be as inconsequential as not being sincere when they said hello to the mail man or maybe watching too much TV. Regardless, the same set of principles apply. These lessons can last a lifetime. Don't let the guilt hinder you. Let it be a motivator to being a better person.

It's also possible that you may have done something so awful that some people will never forgive you. The same applies here. The past is the past and the future is wide open. You must learn from your mistakes if you are to be a better person. You will have to move on and show that you can do something good. You may not be forgiven and you may not win over any fans but you'll know that you succeeded in making a change.

Of course, let's not have any misunderstandings here. I'm not saying that you should forget about what you did. What I'm saying is rather than let an event be the point at which your life turned, let it be the point at which your life *turned around*. Nobody is perfect, but we can try to do our best by ourselves and our fellow human beings.

Guilt should be a learning tool, not a crutch to be unhappy. We're no good to anyone if we sit around, incapacitated over stuff that we may or may not have done. Just like you can't live in the future, you can't live in the past either. Cut loose that albatross and try to do your best in the present. The future and the past will take care of themselves.

You can't be a martyr.

We all know them and we all are annoyed by them. Martyrs make us all sick to our stomachs.

You may not recognize them by this name, but, rest assured, you know exactly who I'm talking about. Remember how when you went home at Thanksgiving and your mother whined and complained about all the hard work she had done preparing dinner, yet refused your offer to help? She was acting the martyr. Remember when that woman at work offered to work over on something that wasn't even her job just for the sake of complaining about it later? She was acting the martyr.

You think that I'm probably only talking about other people here, but you know that I'm talking about you as well. We all have a bit of the martyr in us, there's no question. We all want people to feel sorry about our sad, pitiful plight sometimes. The problem comes when we act on it and some of us act on it at any given opportunity. This is absolutely wrong and there's no way that you will ever be happy if you act the martyr. Remember, martyrs are supposed to be pitied. If they're happy, then they wouldn't be martyrs, would they?

I'm sure that you'll probably read this and say to yourself that you never, ever do anything like this. You're always strong, stoic and always willing to shoulder that burden without any thought or need of recognition, right?

Gotcha! If you think this way, you're being a martyr. It's okay to think this way. Everybody wants to evoke that little tear every once in a while. Just stop yourself before it gets to be a problem.

The sad thing about martyrs is that most people don't even recognize them as such and there are some opportunistic individuals who will even seek them out. This is especially true in the workplace. Have you ever noticed how hard work can be its own reward? Have you ever noticed that if you're a hard worker, then you will work hard? Well, these same principles apply to martyrs. A person who willingly takes on lots of work just to elicit the sympathy of the team will inevitably end up doing that hard work without one iota of genuine appreciation. It will become expected and no one will feel sorry for him. The person's self-sacrificing will be taken for granted and will be expected the next go around.

As for your parents, they probably have more of a reason to play the martyrs, but don't let them get away with it too much otherwise you will never be able to go to any family functions without becoming angry. All you have to do is to call them on it. When they say they don't need any help, go ahead and help. If they say that they don't need you to do anything, do it anyway. And if all this fails, just bring it out into the open. You'll be surprised at how mom's hateful behavior will change once you ask her why she insists on playing the martyr.

Playing the martyr may seem like a good idea on some levels, but not if you actually want to be happy. People will either resent or take advantage of you. Because of this, it's just not a good idea to start playing this role. So, the next time, you feel like doing a little self-sacrificing at the office or over the holidays, just remember that while you may get to lord your martyrdom over everybody, you still end up doing all the work.

This is definitely something to think about.

Happy people don't hold grudges.

This one is tough for most people. I know that I'm no exception. Sometimes it's extremely hard to let go of an old hurt. But if you are going to be truly happy, you're going to have to rise above. You're going to have to transcend petty hurts and jealousies and move on with your life.

Like everything, it's easier said than done. Letting go of a grudge is one of the hardest things that you'll ever do. As humans we all have a survival instinct and I'm of the opinion that these grudges are a part of that. Somebody does us wrong, we get even. Either that or we are constantly vigilant so that they can't do it again. This is not necessarily a bad thing, but when it consumes you, it can be terrible.

For example, when I was in school, I had a friend whose girlfriend was stolen by another one of my friends. Since I was an outside observer, I had information regarding the situation that he didn't. Namely, that the girlfriend was as much a pursuer as a pursuee. In other words, the relationship was over and the fact that she left him for another fellow was just a minor detail. Obviously enough, my friend absolutely hated the guy who "stole" his girlfriend and no amount of my telling him about his girlfriend's involvement would change his view of things. He couldn't even hear the guy's name without going into a rage. After a while, he even went so far as acting like everything was okay so that he would get an opportunity to hang out with the "girlfriend-thief" just to get a clear opportunity to pound him. He was miserable and probably still is to this day and it's been over many, many years since it happened. He has never moved on and I don't think he every will. He just couldn't get over the grudge. On a side note, he did later reunite with the girl only to be dumped yet again six months later for another guy. Oddly enough, his grudge didn't carry over to the new offender.

While the story of my friend may be an extreme case, we all have people who just make us irritable. We can think back to a single situation and get so mad that we could just about boil an egg on our heads. This isn't healthy, but sometimes it's hard to do any better than that. It's good to stay wary, but don't let your grudge consume you. Don't let it be the focal point of your life and above all, don't cheat yourself out of happiness because you would rather spend your time obsessing about what some jerk is doing.

But what if you can't let go? What if you've tried everything possible and still can't get over your grudge? Well, be happy that you're at least recognizing that you are holding grudges. This is a good step in the right direction. It may even be possible that you won't ever be able to let your grudge go, but you can at least try. And if you can't let your grudge go, at least control it. You can do this by rationalizing the situation. You should think about just how much time and energy you're wasting on someone you don't even like. You'll see that the grudge isn't really worth the effort.

When you actively hold a grudge you're only wasting time and energy that could be better spent on something you enjoy more.

So you've wasted your life, huh?

As the old saying goes, there's only two things that are for certain and that's death and taxes. Well, I would like to add another one. It's the fact that no matter what you're able to accomplish in life, there will never be enough time to do everything that you want to do. At least if you're not lying to yourself, that is.

All too often, I see people who deny themselves this or that because they haven't done x y or z. They can't get married until they back pack across Europe. They can't have a kid until they've written their first novel and on and on. I'm here to tell you that this is no way to live life. You're just going to have to get used to the fact that you'll always feel like you've wasted your life regardless of what you do. This is because we are naturally conscientious beings. We always think that we could've done more. We could've made more of ourselves. I would be willing to guarantee that the richest man in the world will have regrets on his death bed.

So, what's the solution?

There's no solution. That's the solution. As I say repeatedly through this book, if you are to live a happy life, you're just going to have to resign yourself to the fact that you'll feel like this when you get older. And fact of the matter is, as hard as this may be to swallow, that you probably could've done more with your life. However, as long as you do your best, you'll be okay. This approach has done wonders for my mental well-being.

It's just a natural trait that you'll feel like you either haven't done enough or that you've wasted your life when you get older. The only solution is to resign yourself to this fact. Recognition of the situation makes it much easier to deal with. Also, make sure that you do your best in everything at the time you're do it and you'll at least know that you did that. Stop second guessing yourself and follow your instincts and you'll be all right. Remember, your best is all that you can do and if you do that, then what more could you have done? It answers a lot of difficult questions and that's a pretty good feeling.

Drawn to those who reject you. The human conundrum.

You know that you do it. No? Liar. Everyone does. We just can't get enough of the people who reject us in relationships.

For some reason, the more we are rejected by a person the more we desire to be with them. We long for them all the more when they ignore us. It shows us to be the absolutely pathetic people that we are. I don't know why, but this is true. While it seems to be a natural trait for us, it only serves to make us unhappy.

The bottom line when we love someone who hates us, we usually only end up hating ourselves.

So, what's the solution?

I don't see one. Just like all the other things that make us unhappy, it's just a naturally occurring situation. Cervantes even wrote about it in *Don Quixote.* We're always drawn to the ones who don't like us that much. The only suggestion I have is to recognize when we're making a fool of ourselves over someone who isn't interested. Sometimes, it's hard to do this because, many times, the person we're fawning over doesn't know we like him/her. If this is the case, take a chance and ask the person out. If he/she says no, then you know that you tried. You can move and stop obsessing. If we can see when we're being absolutely pathetic in our attempts to woo over the un-woo-able, then maybe we'll put the brakes on it a lot sooner and save ourselves a lot of unhappiness.

Conversely, there may be some good that may come from this foolishness in that while we are at our unhappiest when others reject us, we are at our happiest when others accept us. This is why it feels so good to be in a good relationship.

So, if a person doesn't like you, move on. Don't make yourself unhappy over someone who doesn't care. The role of the tragic victim is rarely well-rewarded. However it does rank right up there with being pathetic.

You're stronger than you think.

Being happy is not has hard as you think. You only have to let yourself. I know how everybody says that you are your own obstacle and I strongly agree with that. Are your problems really so bad that you'll never be over them? Are you such a basket-case that there's absolutely no hope? The one thing I've noticed among unhappy people is that happiness isn't the only thing they're lacking. Another thing that has somehow managed to elude their possession is perspective. If you can just step back and take an objective look at yourself, you'll see that no matter how bad you have it, there's somebody else who has it a lot worse. And also there are people who have it a lot worse who are a lot happier than you. Their attitude is better because they know that the hard times will pass. They know that good things can happen.

So this is my advice to you: The next time you find yourself feeling down, ask yourself why you feel this way. Is it because you're delaying your gratification? Is it because you doubt yourself? Is it because you're comparing yourself to other people? Is it because you feel helpless? Is it because you can't accept the fact that you're not in control? Regardless of what your problem is, if you'll just ask yourself this one question, it'll help you put things into a little bit of perspective. Ask yourself, "*One hundred years from now, is anybody going to care about my problems?*"

Just think about this question and you'll see what I'm talking about because if you think about it, no matter what's going on with you now, it'll be long forgotten or at least just a footnote in the future. The fact of the matter is that no one will really care about your problems then. So why not take this view point now and move on? There's nothing stopping you from being happy now except your problems and once you get your perspective straight, they'll be a piece of cake.

So why can't you just be happy?

While I hope that this book points you in the right direction, the answer is ultimately up to you. Just please keep in mind, regardless of what you've gone through in life, you can be happy because you are stronger than you think.

CPSIA information can be obtained at www.ICGtesting.com
Printed in the USA
LVOW07s2055190115

423463LV00001B/37/P

9 781932 420326